Saving Grandmother's Face

Saving Grandmother's Face

And Other Tales from Christian Teachers in China

AMINTA ARRINGTON

EDITOR

RESOURCE *Publications* · Eugene, Oregon

SAVING GRANDMOTHER'S FACE
And Other Tales from Christian Teachers in China

Resource Publications
An Imprint of Wipf and Stock Publishers
199 W. 8th Ave., Suite 3
Eugene, OR 97401
www.wipfandstock.com

ISBN 13: 978-1-60899-043-6

Manufactured in the U.S.A.

Contents

Foreword

IF I REMEMBER CORRECTLY, the first time I supported a Westerner planning to teach in China was back in July 1980—even before I had made my first trip to China. It happened when I was assisting the beloved retired missionary of the China Inland Mission, Dr. David Adeney. However, all I could do then was join David in prayer for this pioneering and dedicated ESL teacher. Neither David nor I knew what teaching in China would be like or for what the teacher and his dear wife should prepare. China had just opened up to the outside world and this Christian teacher, who had previously taught in Japan, took the first bold step of responding to UCLA's advertisement and heading for Beijing with our excitement and blessings.

Time has flown, and as this book is being published in 2010, I am in my twenty-third year of placing Christian teachers in Chinese universities. ERRC (Educational Resources & Referrals—China) placed its first team of foreign teachers in one of China's leading universities in the summer of 1987, with assistance from the Foreign Expert Bureau of the State Council (now the State Administration of the Foreign Expert Affairs, SAFEA).

Many people have asked me if I get bored after twenty-three years of the same work. My answer is that I have never felt that my work has been repetitious—because every year something is new, different, and unpredictable. Even though there are routines to follow, there are always surprises and uncontrollable elements in placing our teachers. Overall, it is a journey of faith year after year. How can seeing 200-plus dedicated Christian teachers serving God in China year after year be boring?

The Lord has given ERRC the opportunities to place teachers in the leading universities in China, and the Lord has also given ERRC talented and outstanding Christian teachers. Our teachers range from retired academic deans, university department chairs, and city mayors to retired Iraq officials, veteran marines, and army soldiers. Each ERRC teacher has a wonderful story of how the Lord led him or her to China. Each person's experience in China is full of stories too. Many of our teachers are excellent writers and offer insightful observations, stories of teaching and learning, and thoughtful reflections. Reading their stories has been a treat to me.

Aminta Arrington, who has been teaching with ERRC since 2006 and who is a keen and passionate cross-cultural observer, initiated the idea of collecting ERRC teachers' stories into a book two years ago. She volunteered to select and edit the pieces for this volume. We appreciate her willingness and her joy in this work.

I cannot imagine how Aminta—a mother of three young children and a full-time English teacher—has had the time and energy to accomplish this project. With her compassionate heart, open mind, and keen curiosity, she not only has written her own stories but also edited the stories of her like-minded colleagues. We appreciate her dedication and meticulous work.

Living cross-culturally has its challenges. However, many ERRC teachers have not only survived in China, they have also soared in China. I do admire them. Their creativity, wisdom, humility, and resilience are testimonies of God's faithfulness and grace. Through God's enabling, these talented writers and committed teachers have embraced a culturally and linguistically alienating world in order to build meaningful friendships, to share common human experiences, and to grow in God's grace. Their writing is a gift.

I respect the courage and faith of all ERRC teachers who have stepped forth in boldness to teach in China. Each teacher has passion— a passion for God, for His kingdom, for Chinese people, and for their deep yielding for growing and giving. Such passion produces its own reward—not a reward of fruit to be counted, but instead a close walk with God. The lives of our teachers are powerful testimonies among their students. The fruits have grown out of trees planted by streams of water (Psalm 1).

This book not only will encourage more Christians to boldly step across cultures—it also will serve as a milestone of ERRC's ministry in China. May the Lord use this book beyond our imagination for His kingdom.

The world is getting smaller, and China is growing closer to the West. How do we encounter China in the twenty-first century? I hope these ERRC teachers' stories will provide inspiration. Not one of these writers is a perfect or heroic figure. However, at some point, each made a decision—a decision to make a difference in his or her own life and a decision to make a difference in other people's lives. God has used them as His instruments for His good work. (II Timothy 2: 20-21).

I have matured from that young woman who prayed with that pioneering teacher to China back in 1980, and so has ERRC. I will use the rich experiences and affirmations in this book to challenge and welcome others to join us at ERRC. Let us hear your story next.

Martha Chan
Founding President
Educational Resources and Referrals—China

Preface

IN THE FALL OF 2008 I was sitting in a small apartment in China with fellow teachers—most of whom my colleagues from ERRC—when I was simultaneously struck by two realizations. First, many of them were excellent writers. Second, their writings about China were fundamentally different from mainstream media accounts. For while newspapers and the Internet are filled with headlines about China—its rise on the world stage, the abuses of its authoritarian political system, its factories that produce so many of the products we buy every day—few pieces dig into the culture and history of this fascinating country. And even fewer examine China from a Christian worldview.

I realized then that these teachers had experienced life in China on a level that was not usually written about. They had befriended Chinese—students, shopkeepers, taxi drivers—who rarely had their stories told. I knew that my colleagues not only could, but ought to, write a book. I mentioned the thought to Martha Chan, ERRC's president. She promptly asked me to edit such a book and found a publisher.

And thus we have *Saving Grandmother's Face and other Tales from Christian Teachers in China*. The essays in this book are diverse. Some reflect experiences in the classroom. Others are travel adventures to remote villages or fantastic landscapes. Still others describe the frustrations and joys of learning Chinese. The essays reflect cultural experiences ranging from childbirth to funerals. Some are written by new teachers struggling to adapt to a new culture; others by seasoned teachers still learning.

Common to every essay is the idea of transformation—the unavoidable change when a Western teacher meets this ancient Eastern culture. Long-held beliefs and unexamined convictions are put to the test. I hope that these essays will challenge their readers to likewise examine previously unchallenged assumptions.

This book is about the ordinary Chinese people with whom we teachers interact, so for the most part, it stays away from broader political themes. And while as Christian teachers we recognize the work that God is doing in China, this remains a sensitive area and therefore is not the topic of this book.

A volume like this is not possible without the work of many hands. Most of the credit goes to the teachers who took time away from their primary work—in the classroom and relating with students—to write about their experiences. Rob Moore wrote the contributor biographies in a way that was light-hearted and humorous, yet still informative. Sharon Seeberger and Sharon Steinmiller provided extra pairs of editing eyes. Sheryl Smalligan edited so thoroughly and painstakingly she rendered a copy-edit unnecessary. Finally, Martha Chan recognized the importance of this volume, recommended the outstanding writers among ERRC teachers, and provided encouragement while continuing to lead ERRC, the organization that fostered such freedom and creativity.

Aminta Arrington
Tai'an, Shandong Province, China
March 2010

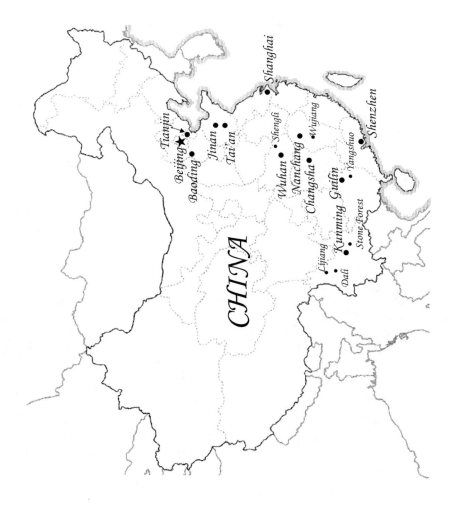

1

Saving Grandmother's Face

by Don and Karen Barnes

TRADITIONAL CHINESE CULTURE ATTACHES great importance to the family. The ideal family exhibits certain admirable qualities and behaviors, such as respect for elders, familial loyalty, and other wholesome Confucian traits. In the ideal family, life's rituals are carried out in appropriate forms and rhythms. For example, there is an appropriate/auspicious time to be born, to be married, to have children, and even to die.

But life can be complex, and sometimes glitches cause life to deviate from the ideal. When that happens, a little creative tinkering may be necessary in order to maintain the proper form. And herein lies the tale.

In this case, our new friend had a grandmother who had lived a long and fruitful life. As she neared the end of her sojourn on earth, she reviewed her affairs to see that everything was in order. Decisions had been made about many items, such as the disposition of her worldly goods, the distribution of her family responsibilities, and the details of her burial, including the grave marker, what we would call the tombstone.

While almost everything was in order, the tombstone presented a real problem. You see, in traditional Chinese culture, one's tombstone should display the essential information about the deceased, including the deceased's name, the names of her offspring, and the names of her grandchildren.

It was at this point that modern life had gotten out of rhythm in this particular case. Grandmother had nobly fulfilled her responsibilities by bearing a number of children, including sons. However, the sons had tarried in getting married so that there were no grandchildren when

Grandmother was about to expire. In the Chinese culture of that time (circa 1960), having no names of grandchildren on the tombstone was a big problem of form and face. It just wouldn't do for Grandmother to leave the earth with nothing but blanks on this critical portion of her tombstone.

Being unable to hasten the conception, gestation, and birthing processes, the family resorted to other means to address this problem. Specifically, they called in the local religious monks in order to gain their insights about the future births that would surely come to the sons (and their wives) some day. In particular, the monks were asked to predict the number and gender of the grandchildren who would be born at some point in the future.

The monks plied their trade with due diligence and fervent honesty. Finally, they received the revelation that the sons would have three daughters among them at some point in the future.

On the basis of this prediction by authoritative sources, the family rejoiced and came up with three girls' names to inscribe on Grandmother's tombstone that would represent the granddaughters who were bound to come.

Reassured that everything was now in order, Grandmother passed away, satisfied that proper form had been followed—sort of—and that the family traditions had been upheld sufficiently to meet the spirit, if not the letter, of the ritual.

Time passed and, as predicted by the monks, the sons got down to business and produced three bouncing baby . . . errr . . . uh-oh . . . boys. Yes, boys, not the daughters that had been predicted. However, the die had been cast—the tombstone was already carved with three girls' names and was on public display. Therefore, in order to make an honest woman of Grandmother—but with some hesitance and more embarrassment—the three boys were legally given the girls' names that were on Grandmother's tombstone. To do otherwise would have brought shame and discredit to the poor woman, and such a loss of face—even for the deceased—was unthinkable.

Today, the three grandsons, in fact, have given names that are traditionally female names. However, in order to save *their* face and to spare themselves the inevitable razzing that would ensue, they seldom, if ever, share this bit of family history. In fact, long ago they took for their daily use names that are unequivocally masculine, and it is by these names that most of the world knows them.

How do we know that this story is true? It was told to us by the *fourth* grandchild to be born into the family, who was, therefore, safely beyond the reach of the "female moniker curse" of Grandmother's tombstone and whose given name is legally and safely—and manly—Peter.

Mountains, Water

山水

by Aminta Arrington

*The river forms a green gauze belt;
the mountains are like blue jade hairpins.*

—Han Yu, Tang Dynasty poet, of Guilin

I RECOGNIZE NOW THAT my interest in China started with Guilin. More specifically, it started when I watched the movie *The Joy Luck Club*, based on the novel by Amy Tan. The year was 1994. I drove from North Carolina, where I was living after graduation from college, to Atlanta to meet some old college friends. I walked into a movie theater with my girlfriends, having no idea of what I was about to watch. I sat spellbound. This tale of Chinese-born mothers, their American-born daughters, and their mutual frustration at not being able to relate to one another at times completely captured me.

The movie went back to when the mothers were young, living in China, and suffering as only Chinese who have lived through the war and upheaval of the early twentieth century know suffering. In one flashback, a Chinese woman trudges along in a long line of refugees fleeing war. She struggles to put one foot in front of the other as she pushes a wheelbarrow with two bundled-up babies, her twin daughters. Afflicted by dysentery and other maladies, she expects she will die. To save her daughters from the bad luck of being found with their dead mother, she abandons them by the side of the road, leaving a note as well as jewelry and anything else valuable she has.

Besides the poignancy of this scene, I was equally moved by the scenery. Particularly, the mountains. They speared straight up out of the ground like teeth poking out of gums. Was this scenery real or just a Hollywood invention? I had no idea that such landscape even existed.

I harbored this image in my mind for years. While living in Japan, my interest in China was renewed, culminating in the adoption of our daughter Grace. But in the nascent stages, when I was still a student at Waseda University in Tokyo, I described this scenery to my Chinese classmates. "Ah yes," they nodded knowingly, "Guilin."

At last the image had a name. Guilin.

Guilin was the only place that fascinated me simply for its landscape. I am just not that much into scenery. I get more excited about culture and people. That's why I like to go places. But Guilin was all about the scenery. I just had to see those mountains. No other scenery has had such a hold on me as Guilin, and for so many years.

When we were in the process of adopting Grace, I would daydream that she was from Guilin, thinking it would be quite a poetic ending if the daughter of my dreams were from the landscape of my dreams. But in fact Grace was from Jiangxi, a province I had never heard of and had a hard time finding on a map. As we planned our adoption trip, I thought about adding a side trip to Guilin, but finances precluded that, as they had on my earlier trip to China.

Now we were living in China, and planning our trip to southern climes for the winter semester break. Since we were already down south with our travels to Thailand and Hainan Island, my husband Chris insisted we take a side trip to Guilin. As I made the flight arrangements, I could see it would be more convenient to fly through Kunming, and I suggested to him that instead we see Kunming, since we had to go through that airport anyway. But he insisted we see Guilin.

"You've been talking about this for so long, as long as we've been together. We just need to go to Guilin to fulfill your dream (and to get you to shut up about it!)"

With that kind of personal history, Guilin had a lot to live up to. We flew in after nightfall. I strained my eyes looking for their forms, but the mountains were invisible, cloaked in darkness. I awoke in the hotel room the next morning, opened my eyes, and quickly drew the drapes.

I was not disappointed. The mountains jutted upward right from the street, vertically, like pencils with worn-down erasers. The hazy forms of my memory turned into solid bedrock right outside my window.

On the agenda for that day was the Li River cruise, a must on any tourist trip to Guilin. The mountains formed a crowd at the riverbank—standing room only. One was so perfectly cylindrical it looked like a prehistoric giant had made it using a prehistoric oversize soup can. Another looked like a camel with seven or eight humps. I enjoyed the scenery immensely. But there were a lot of distractions. The river was saturated with tourist vessels, and we were never free from vendors.

While we were cruising, a man in one of the Phoenix Tail Bamboo rafts typical of Guilin pulled up to the side of the ferry. The raft was a single layer of bamboo poles, tied together and rising at one end. I watched the man curiously, wondering what he was doing. I decided he must be attaching himself to the boat as a means of hitching a ride downstream. Grabbing on near the bow, he gradually made his way back until he reached the first window, ours. I pointed him out to the kids, showing them the raft and pointing out the bamboo. As if on cue, he smiled and waved. I was pleased. We smiled and waved back. He then opened the crate in the center of his raft, withdrew some items, and with a flick of his wrist displayed a fan painted with Guilin scenery. He was a vendor. And I, innocently, had allowed my guard to drop.

The raft vendors accompanied us the rest of the way downstream. Passengers, if interested, would open their windows and the bargaining would begin over carved frogs, crystals, stones, and other trinkets.

After the cruise, we headed to Yangshuo. I had added Yangshuo to the itinerary after hearing a snippet of conversation in which one of our colleagues mentioned that Yangshuo was a nicer place to visit than Guilin. That turned out to be great advice, for we thoroughly enjoyed this small town.

One guidebook aptly described Yangshuo as having an "international, bohemian atmosphere."

"This place is great," Chris said. "I could just hang out here." We loved it from the first moment, walking from our hotel to West Street, a pedestrian street filled with sidewalk cafes, clothing stores, local gift stores, and art galleries containing scroll after scroll painted with Guilin's famous scenery.

In Chinese, this scenery is dubbed 山水, literally "mountains, water." This is a typical Chinese linguistic pattern: choosing two characters to denote the boundaries of a concept. Here it refers to landscape containing both mountains and water and everything in between.

We spent the next morning in a private calligraphy lesson arranged by our guide. The girls and I had great fun practicing the strokes, numbers, and a few basic characters. Chris videotaped and took pictures while our son Andrew sat at his own desk immersed in a book.

山

mountains

For the afternoon, we were scheduled to take a bicycle tour of the countryside. The kids couldn't ride yet, but Chris offered to take care of them in the hotel room so that I could go.

"Are you sure?" I asked him.

"It's no problem. I'm just riding along anyway, facilitating your dream."

So Cherry, our guide, John, a fellow teacher, and I rented bikes on West Street, then headed out of town. Our first stop was a farmer's house. The 71-year-old woman of the house was our hostess. Her husband also peeked in briefly.

水

water

She served us a pomelo, similar to a gigantic grapefruit, grown herself. As we peeled the thick membranes from each segment of pomelo to reveal the delicious interior, a large portrait of Chairman Mao looked down at us from the living room wall. To his left and right were red paper couplets with large Chinese characters, though the woman explained that she, illiterate, could not read them.

After we had eaten, she led us into the courtyard, the centerpiece of her 340-year-old home, where we washed our hands using water from the hand pump. The kitchen, an outbuilding next to the courtyard, consisted of a low cement counter with two holes for woks and charcoal fires underneath.

We returned to the living area via a side room. There she presented two wooden rectangular boxes: coffins. Her children had purchased them about eight months previously, she informed us. She lifted the lid of one and proudly showed us the inside.

Our guide explained that this was Chinese custom. In fact, it was the duty of children to buy their parents coffins and for the parents to approve. This was a way of expressing care and fidelity.

"In this way, they know everything is taken care of," she explained. I immediately wondered what my parents would think if I suggested such a coffin-buying shopping trip.

I also wondered what it must be like to live in my house with my own coffin, which I would inevitably inhabit one day—to walk by it day in and day out. How would this affect my life? Would it make the menial tasks of the day, still important to this elderly farming couple, seem trivial? My Western mind had a hard time grasping how the presence of these coffins could be comforting to the elderly couple, as our guide explained that it was.

From the farmhouse we bicycled to a small tributary of the Li River, where we boarded a two-seater bamboo raft, our bikes tied to the back. The limestone karst mountains seemed even more fantastic and distinct than the day before, and there was nothing to do on the raft but take them in. The mountains were visible in layers, the farther ranges visible between the nearer and gradually fading into lighter shades of blue, like rows of hunched animals. The raft master, perched on the back, steered us with the help of a long bamboo pole, along the way navigating three or four small dams. He pointed out key scenery along the way, exhorting us at times to lift our legs to avoid getting our feet soaked.

On the Li River cruise the day before I had been too distracted by kids, as well as by other tourists, vendors, and passing boats to really take in the scenery. But this time only a layer of bamboo separated me from the water, only fresh air separated me and the mountains. I finally felt I had truly breathed in the 山水.

3

Renovation

by Amanda Hostetler

I't's hot here tonight as I write. Someone finally remembered to turn on the heat lamp in our city of Wuhan, called "The Furnace" of China. The children have been restless and asking for air conditioning, as the evening cool is ever so tardy. As I sit up trying to be still, swatting at thirsty mosquitoes, it begins again—my mind begins to churn with images of what I've seen here and what I "knew" in my life before China. I realize that my very foundation is being excavated.

My husband and I lived for six years in an old farmhouse that had been ill-fated to a life of half-hearted devotion on the part of its owners. When we took possession, we were shocked to find that for its first eighty-three years of life, no drywall or plaster had ever covered the ship-lathe walls upstairs. They were, in fact, adorned with only wallpaper hung over old burlap feed sacks that had been nailed to the wood slats with rusty roofing nails. For all the years it stood before our ownership and sadly during the years we inhabited it, the house was never "finished." We joked that it was under constant renovation.

It would be an understatement to say that living in a home under renovation is not fun. After ten months of living abroad, I have discovered that living with a mind that is forcibly under renovation is at times even less pleasant.

Of course, I knew that, in coming to China, we would be stretching our lives and experiences far outside what we'd known as "normal" and that our thinking would inevitably change. However, I've stumbled upon a revelation regarding my previous mental practices. With the benefit of

20/20 hindsight, I see that prior to moving to China, I did precious little independent thinking.

While I was firmly ensconced in my version of the American Dream, I moved within an atmosphere of opinion, idealism, and information gluttony. Whether listening to talk radio, engaging in random discussions around town, tuning in to an infrequent newscast, or gazing at the magazine covers at the grocery store check-out, I was deluged with the noise of commentary (even *without* a subscription to cable television). In that environment, my mind coasted along, as idle as any flabby couch potato and engorged with someone else's intellectual process. Critical thinking, the fiber of a sound mind, was not part of my mental diet. I consumed others' points of view as my own and over time got used to the mass-produced ideologies that were like warmed-up Salisbury steak TV dinners. After a while one is convinced that TV dinners are real food that can nurture cerebral fitness.

For me, living in China without command of the language, the fountain of attainable information has slowed to a trickle. There is so little conversation available for me to absorb that my mind has begun to consider the world around me, with curiosity. Initially I experienced a generalized anxiety from the sensation of wheels turning in my mind. The ideas that rose to my consciousness seemed risky and unproven. Alas, they were not vetted by the talking heads in my previous sphere of experience—instead they were virgin and quite alarmingly not attributable to anyone but me. But, to my astonishment, my synapses have slowly begun to fire with free thought.

I'm reading several books right now. Of course along with the absence of intelligible language comes the opportunity to feast on heartier fare for my brain. The first book is an extremely strident wake-up call to Christians in the West, authored by a man who lived in the East and suffered enormous persecution. The second was written some years ago by an intellectual from China as his dissertation on the mindset of the East versus the West. The two books, on some matters, are diametrically opposed. Yet both leave me with a gnawing awareness that my fuzzy, sugar-coated worldview requires demolition and the laying of a surer foundation.

Growing up in the Midwest, even though I would never have admitted it (and in fact internally boasted of being unencumbered by culturally-biased thinking), I was entrenched in my simplistic constructs of life, faith, and humankind. I fancied myself not one of "those" who were limited to a narrow worldview. While I was drawn to everything and anyone exotic in the community, in fact the fruit of my mindset fell only a slight distance from the tree where I had grown.

Living in China, we are pressed in on all sides by humanity. I am often so close to another human being on the bus riding to town that I feel I should confess something untoward to my husband upon my return! My mind is constantly processing the masses that I see each day through the filter of my Western, middle-class background. Yet the longer I live here, the more I am confronted with the limitations I've had on my thinking and how I believe He wants me to have a greater scope, and more generous eyes, more like His. The little boxes where I had previously filed things, especially God, are utterly useless and inadequate. I recognize my need to surrender further to the Holy Spirit, so I can begin to experience a migration toward renewed sight, sight akin to His.

Just this evening my eyes fell upon two farmers, in their manicured field, squatting down to diligently work their crops. They sweated over neat raised rows of brilliant green plantings, their bare feet caked with the ruddy earth. They'd fashioned some sort of over-sized parasol that jutted out of the ground to shield them from the merciless sun. Who are they? What is their story? Have they experienced love? Rapidly my mind began to create a story for them. Then I was simultaneously chagrined as I realized the story I concocted for them exposed my own rose-colored view of what a "hard day" was like.

A bit later as we drove down a city street, I spotted a young man, his auto-repair shop a scanty stall in a row of similar enterprises. He was sitting on his heels, filthy and covered in grease, working on an engine block out in the road. Stalled in the anarchy of a Chinese traffic jam, the smell of oil and solvents intertwined in the humid air and made my throat feel thick and sore. As the cars crawled on, the disagreeable breathing conditions trailing behind me, I considered the mechanic. What does he dream about? What does he need? Has anyone taken the time to know him and share his or her heart with him? In my Father's eyes, he is of equal value to me, loved and longed for by a Savior. Do I really care?

A few years ago my husband traveled to India with a Christian humanitarian organization. Among the more than one thousand pictures he brought back was one that produced a seminal moment for me. It remains a moment to which I look back and see an instigation of awareness. The photo disturbed me deeply and aroused a realization of my truly pretentious understanding of hardship. It illuminated at my core a general lack of compassion.

This excerpt is from my journal in January 2007:

There's just one picture that I cannot get out of my mind—the lady in the street. She's sitting in the street, begging, her son curled up and sleeping with his head on her lap.

Of course, I don't know if he was sleeping. I assumed so because I'm an American who thinks that living in suburbia without a husband who is traveling for twelve days is a real hardship. Maybe the boy wasn't sleeping at all? Perhaps he was just too weak or too hungry to sit up next to her and beg? It's hard for my mind to conceive of anything like that. My healthy, well fed children are so loud playing in the next room I am unable to construct such a reality, even in my imagination.

My husband apologized for the resolution of the photograph. He said it didn't fully tell the story. He was riding in a bus and shot the picture through the glass. You see, the picture didn't capture the tears that he saw streaming down her cheeks while she was sitting in the middle of the busy, overcrowded road, her son's head in her lap.

Should I be angry at myself for not understanding her reality? Should I chastise myself for not being able to relate to what that life would be like sitting IN THE STREET . . . weeping . . . begging . . . with a child huddled next to me?

In America, we get mad about noisy neighbors who don't weed their flower beds. We're irate over some comment that a pinhead on the nightly news has made. We're so frustrated with slow-moving traffic that traps us in our climate-controlled vehicle for a few more minutes. We're so very busy navel gazing and lamenting about how unfulfilled we are and wonder when it will be time for "us."

How could I relate? The abundance in which I live is like the Novocain my dentist uses before he drills on my teeth. The greater the abundance, the less I feel anything, especially compassion and connection with an unfortunate woman weeping in the street on the other side of the world.

If I had been there, if I had seen her would I even have anything to say to her? Could I even open my mouth in her presence? Maybe I'll just delete the picture and go back to worrying about that car repair that needs to be done. Now that's a real pain . . .

How foolish I've been . . .

I am thankful for the seed that picture planted in my life. At that time, I had no idea that our family would be called to move from the West to live in China. Now some three and a half years later, living in this new culture, I can see that my mind still employs duplicitous techniques to screen out the unpleasant realities of those around me. Yet I am hopeful that as my psyche has begun to generate ideas on its own and while I partner that with the discipline of applying the teachings of Christ, I might arrest my simplistic and self-centered perspective and grow in His love and compassion for every man, woman, and child.

Recently, my husband and I enjoyed a discussion with a dear Chinese friend who, like us, is growing and searching for more meaningful answers. We talked about the Eastern mindset and the Western one and what his impressions were of the differences between our young nation's history and his country's ancient one. We theorized about the role of Christianity as a foundation for a government and economic system. He enlightened us further about the merits of Confucianism. It was an encouraging exchange as we were able to experience our common humanity that bridged our diverse cultural roots.

We talked about the Christians in China and the brothers and sisters in the United States. He asked about the passion of those who follow Jesus in the West—is it as great as he imagines?

What could I answer?

When I replied that universal fire and zeal were not necessarily the hallmarks with which I would describe much of the Church in the West, he replied, "Ah, things that are easy to get are easy to lose."

Perhaps that brings me back to the initial premise of this writing. It would seem that every brick of "truth" that I hastily grabbed to form my early foundation is now being challenged and examined. If I say that love is in my foundation, then does that brick hold up under the pressure of the uncomfortable culture-stress of my day-to-day existence? If not, I must renovate! I must replace that easily acquired brick with one that is divinely constructed to withstand any shaking that life in a new culture brings with it.

Is compassion more than a buzzword in the arsenal of adjectives I use to describe my core? If it is, then it should be clearly evidenced in my daily existence as surely as my DNA is manifested in my brown eyes. Every brick that I have prided myself upon in my sure foundation must be inspected, lest my mindset and work on this earth be built upon human conventions and reasoning. As the Apostle Paul instructs in 2 Corinthians 10:5, "We demolish arguments and every pretension that sets itself up against the knowledge of God, and we take captive every thought to make it obedient to Christ."

Only through the vigorous examination of my foundation, scrutinizing it by the illumination of Scripture and dutifully replacing each faulty component, can I realize a transformation of my sight. Such a process allows the scales of my self-absorbed blindness to fall away. It allows my vision to be restored with eyes of compassion and generosity that see those I pass by in the Light of His love, not the vain curiosity of a common observer.

4

Me and Mr. Yang

by Robert Moore

IN CHINESE THERE'S ONLY a minor tonal difference between onion bread (*yóubǐng*) and insanity (*yǒubǐng*). Now the average street vendor will not assume, in the event that you make a mistake, that you are pronouncing yourself crazy when instead you want to order food. But the fact is that with the Chinese language, insanity is never more than a word away. The only people who can properly learn such a language are those who themselves are only a step or two away from, if not insanity, then at least extreme eccentricity. Mr. Yang and I, in the years we knew each other in Tai'an, qualified for both categories. Sometimes our interactions made us merely odd, and sometimes we fed off each other until we were, well, no longer talking about onion bread. So to speak.

I'm sure I'd met Mr. Yang several times before the day he came to his door during the lunch siesta time wearing nothing but his underwear, but then again I may not have. Even if I had, I'm sure the shock of this meeting has blurred the other meetings out of existence. Answering the door in your underwear really isn't too big a deal in China, given that many elderly people regularly take walks in public wearing just their pajamas or long underwear, but where I come from it's slightly on the irregular side. It was my first month in Shandong Province, and I was trying to make a simple instant soup but didn't have any eggs. I went across the hall to ask if I could borrow my missing ingredient. After several seconds Mr. Yang threw open the door.

A preliminary sketch would be in order here. Mr. Yang was of medium height, just slightly shorter than I, with a shock of gray hair set in the classic Mao Zedong-style semicircle. It may just be my imagination, but his hair always seemed to be slightly askew, as though he'd just finished doing feverish research or had just shocked himself on some faulty wiring. He had eyes that went straight past lively and into hyperactivity. Whenever I'd tell him something strange in Chinese or ask him a probing question, he would throw his head back, stare at the ceiling as though trying to burn a hole in it, then throw his hands up as he answered, like a man receiving religious inspiration. He was in stupendous shape, due to his daily routine of swimming in a lake on nearby Mt. Tai, even in winter, and I don't remember ever seeing him tired.

As soon as he saw me, he threw his arms up and, with a loud pronouncement of happiness, invited me to come in. I assured him, as I tried to focus on anything that didn't involve sagging underwear, that I only wanted an egg, and with a clap of his hands he ran off to the kitchen. He returned with the egg and demanded that I come back.

We got to know each other better over the next few weeks, and soon he agreed to start teaching me Chinese. He was also eager to learn English, a declaration which always made his wife cluck her tongue reprovingly. She assured me that her husband was terrible with languages. He began by teaching me how to write. For our first lesson, he brought over a little notebook. It had small grids on the page which enabled the student to make sure every part of the character was in the correct quadrant. We started slowly, he writing each character and me trying to copy it. This didn't work so well because I had no conception of character stroke order and, furthermore, no idea why it was important. I only knew that every time I started drawing a character, he would make a loud "ee!" sound like a hosepipe with an air leak, reach over quickly, and make me start over again. I quickly became annoyed. To me it was like starting to draw a triangle or a square and having someone get angry because I was starting with the wrong side. How can there be a wrong side to a triangle? It's a triangle. It has three sides. That's it. But I ground my teeth and did what he told me. I realized later, of course, that the stroke order is vital because otherwise you can't use a Chinese dictionary, but I didn't learn that for a while. In the meantime our lessons were a succession of sluggish handwriting, numerous leaky hosepipe sounds, and tooth-grinding.

Our spoken Chinese lessons were where Mr. Yang really came into his own. I don't think, even to this day, I've ever met a more animated Chinese person. You'd never know he was in his seventies. Perhaps it was his magnificent choice of undergarments. In any case, he was never boring. Our lessons consisted mostly of my reading slowly through a children's book in Chinese, finding a word I didn't know (which was often), then his trying to explain in broken English. When that failed (as it often did), he would eschew vocal explanation and start pantomiming. To this day, whenever I use the Chinese word for "jump," I remember him illustrating the word by leaping around my living room. "Tiao!" he'd shout and take a massive three-foot leap, landing flat-footed on my floor with a loud smack. Then he'd beam at me, gather up his energy, and do the same thing again. I think he actually made a complete circuit of my living room that way.

He also loved using props, which he inevitably forgot when he left after our lesson. I always knew it was prop time when, after asking him the meaning of a word, he would stare in his rapt way at the ceiling, leap from my sofa and run out of my apartment. I'd hear him open his door with a bang, rummage around, then run back in holding something: a stick, a pair of glasses, a mortar and pestle, whatever.

One day he marched into my apartment and proudly recited, "When you've got to go, you've got to go." For some time he had been reading a little book of English idioms, and he'd made it his mission to memorize a few for each of our lessons. Before we did any Chinese, he would proudly recite what he had learned. The phrases were rarely related and oftentimes completely random. After his proud recital of the common bathroom idiom, I had to fight to keep my composure and explain what the idiom meant. He got the gist of it and laughed. It wasn't an uncomfortable laugh. He was delighted to know something so vulgar. He probably used it around his Chinese friends, cackling away at his own inside joke.

Maybe this was what prompted our bathroom discussion in a later class. Maybe not. Anyway, one day during a lesson I got up to go to the bathroom and just said in Chinese that I had to go.

When I came back, he said, "You know, instead of just saying you're going to the bathroom, you should say what you're doing in there." No I shouldn't, I thought. Not in Chinese culture—and not in any culture, unless it's in a college dorm and you're surrounded by guys for whom the bathroom is less a place of necessity than a recreational zone. But immediately after this he proceeded to teach me *xiao bian* and *da bian*, two Chinese phrases that mean, respectively, "small bathroom" and "big bathroom." Use your imagination. Taking my silence for misunderstanding (it wasn't—I just couldn't think of any appropriate response), he proceeded, yes, to pantomime each action, even going so far as to squat near the floor to illustrate "big bathroom." Part of me was impressed that a man in his seventies was so lithe as to squat, stand, and squat with such fluidity. The rest of me was howling with internal laughter. After his gymnastic demonstration of bathroom vocabulary, he grabbed his little notebook and asked me to write the English translations. The possibility of anyone else's having had to write "pee" and "poop" in an old Chinese man's spiral notebook is remote, so I'll just say here that it's a bizarre experience. It would be bizarre for me to write those words in my own notebook, much less another person's, and certainly when that other person is a foreign language student of any age or nationality. Still, fair is fair. He taught me how to say "pee" and "poop" in Chinese. How could I refuse?

I made my way through several very simple children's books this way. To help supplement my lessons, he began bringing over his granddaughter's old elementary school reading textbook. To my gratitude, he never made me memorize the short poems which all young Chinese students are required to recite. We focused more on the essays. These were an interesting introduction for me to a different aspect of Chinese culture. Several of the readers contained numerous stories of evil Japanese soldiers attacking Chinese people during World War II. I remember thinking it seemed like awfully grisly material for seven-year-olds, but then that would explain much of the vitriolic antipathy against the Japanese of most Chinese people my age or younger. They are literally taught it in school from a young age.

It would be impossible to discuss Mr. Yang without also talking about his wife. Mrs. Yang was the stereotypical image of a Chinese grandmother. She and Mr. Yang were a perfectly-balanced couple: he, loud and gregarious, always in motion—she, quiet and methodical, and kind in a way that only traditional Chinese people are. For as long as I knew her, she was convinced I was going to starve to death.

"You're too thin!" she would crow when she saw me, sometimes lightly smacking my arm. "You should eat more!"

She even took matters into her own hands, and for several weeks sent her husband over during the lunch hour with a plate of food she'd made for me. I once told Mr. Yang that I really didn't eat breakfast regularly. This horrified both him and his wife. So for the next month and some change, Mr. Yang would knock on my door every morning with milk he had bought, milk being the absolute bare minimum of what you should have for breakfast in China in order not to waste away and die by lunch time. I didn't put on much weight. I tried to assure them that this was because I was walking up four flights of stairs several times a day and walking all over town in the meantime, but they just shook their heads. Mrs. Yang lectured me one day and said, "Your mother will see you and become very sad because her son is so thin. I'll have to make sure you get enough food because she isn't here." She certainly did her best.

I ate quite a few meals at their house, all of which were delicious. Mrs. Yang usually spent the entire meal in the kitchen cooking and only joined Mr. Yang and me when everything was finished, and even then she spent most of her time admonishing us to eat more while she picked at a few things. She had learned how to say "Help yourself" in English and proudly used it as often as she could, smiling broadly. A discussion with them was always entertaining during my first year in China because I spoke only snatches of Chinese, and Mr. Yang's English, although certainly better than my Chinese, wasn't fluent. Usually such conversations consisted of Mrs. Yang's first shaking her husband by the shoulder and telling him to ask me something, whereupon he would think for a minute or so and then pop out a translation. I would try to respond in Chinese, but often this resulted in a blank look from Mrs. Yang, who would then shake her husband by the shoulder again to ask for an explanation, thus making each exchange a complete circle. Quite a few times one of them would ask a question, only to be roundly criticized by the other, a state of affairs I understood only when my Chinese improved.

When I came back to visit after having been away from Shandong Province for several years, Mr. Yang gleefully informed me that he was still studying English, a comment that prompted Mrs. Yang to lean towards me slightly and say, "Yes, but he's terrible. He can't speak any English." This just made Mr. Yang laugh. He then went for his *jinghu*, a traditional Chinese instrument, but Mrs. Yang groaned and said, "Don't play that! You're always playing that for guests, and no one ever wants to hear it!" He just laughed and played anyway. She was only ever half-serious about such things, especially the music. One of their traditions was to play Peking Opera together almost every afternoon, with Mr. Yang playing his *jinghu* and Mrs. Yang singing. They never performed for me, though. It was something they did only with their little opera group or in the comfort of their own home. I suppose they felt it was an imposition otherwise.

In addition to all this, I'm fairly certain that had Mrs. Yang not been with him, Mr. Yang would have lost or forgotten everything he ever owned or knew. I've already mentioned his penchant for leaving teaching props in my apartment, but he tended to forget just about everything else too. Once during the middle of winter, he came over for a lesson all bundled up. He had a thick coat and under that a red wool sweater. He was also wearing a hat and carrying a large cup of hot tea. He had his gloves tucked under his arm. My apartment was quite warm, so he deposited most of those items on a chair nearby. We had our lesson, and then he left—and in the process forgot his coat, sweater, hat, gloves, tea, and the little bag containing his notebook. Oblivious, he walked out my door, across the hall, and into his apartment, and from where I was sitting I could hear his wife loudly asking him where all of his warm clothes were. He said, "Oh!" with a loud voice. Then I heard his shuffling footsteps, and in a moment he was with me again, waving sheepishly as he gathered up his things. On another occasion, he was telling me and an American friend about a vacation he and his wife had taken into central and southwestern China.

My friend asked, "So where did you go?"

He thought for a moment, asked us to wait, then ran across the hall, where we heard him and his wife have a brief exchange. Then he ran back and said, "Hunan, Sichuan, and Hubei."

We chatted for a while longer, and then I asked, "How long were you there?"

Again he thought and ran across the hall again. "One month," he replied when he returned.

I would occasionally come upon Mrs. Yang walking slowly around the neighborhood to exercise her sore hip, and if there was a friend with her, she would always insist on introducing me. I made a point of re-introducing Mrs. Yang as my Chinese grandmother, which always made both old women beam. In reality, the affectation was not far from the truth. I became quite good friends with their children, and even with one of their granddaughters, who at the time was in high school. All of them insisted time and time again that I should consider myself a part of the family. I was invited to family gatherings and dinners. During the Mid-Autumn Festival, I was the only non-family guest when the clan went to a restaurant to celebrate. And Mr. Yang felt comfortable enough around me to express things he might not have otherwise. During one of our meals together, when his wife brought in a dish full of food, he looked over at me and said, with a roguish wink, "My wife is very beautiful." The comment earned him a reproving smack on the shoulder from his wife—but then their relationship was always a balance of outlandish behavior and grounded response.

I left Tai'an in 2004, after having lived there for over two years. The night I left, a few people came to see me off, among them my good friend Jiang Zhongai and my dean, Ms. Liu Yan. My students were absent and very apologetic, saying that they were simply too sad and couldn't face seeing me off to the train station. I held my composure pretty well as I piled my things in the back of the taxi, but just before I got in, Mr. Yang and his wife tottered into view. It was much harder saying goodbye to the people who had fed me, taught me, and included me in their family. They, of course, were the typically stoic Chinese couple and merely waved and told me to make sure to come back.

I've seen them a few times since, though not as often as I should have. It's been some time, in fact, since I was able to visit. The last time I was in Tai'an, my Chinese had improved to a point where I could actually talk with them both. They were both ecstatic when I knocked on their door. I was immediately invited to dinner, and Mr. Yang went to call whoever else in the family could come. We were going to meet at a nearby restaurant. Mrs. Yang apologized, saying that her leg hurt so much these days that she found it hard to cook. I assured her going out for dinner was no problem. It wasn't far, so we set out in a small group. Mrs. Yang encouraged me to walk ahead because she was going to be too slow. I waved her off and simply slowed down to walk with her and her husband. Mr. Yang was not in the slightest hurried or annoyed. And so we made our way, with Mrs. Yang setting the pace down the street—an elderly Chinese couple and their odd American grandson.

5

The Funeral

by Samara Sanchez

Tom phoned me on a peaceful Sunday afternoon at a friend's apartment. "Miss Sanchez," he told me, "a boy from Class Seven died suddenly."

Tom was a former student of mine from Beijing who often phoned at random moments to ask me strange questions even after the school year was over and I had moved to Tianjin. "Miss Sanchez," he would ask, "what kind of car did you drive in the U.S.?" Or: "What do you know about public schools in the Chicago area?" At other times he asked me to help him write a speech for a contest and also what he should write in his application essay to a private school in the U.S. I always received these calls at the least convenient times, such as when I was lost looking for an address in the dark or when I was in the market trying to explain something to a merchant. Though in the moment I might have been slightly annoyed, I always finished my conversations with him bemused by his thinking of me as some sort of convenient all-knowing fount of wisdom but yet grateful that one of my former seventh graders was still calling me to let me know what was going on in his eighth grade year.

I asked Tom what had happened. He explained that one day in PE class while the students were stretching—they hadn't even started running yet—his classmate just fell over. The ambulance came and brought him to the hospital, but he didn't make it. No one really knew exactly what had happened, but many people were guessing it had something to do with his heart—a condition no one had suspected. He had seemed to be a healthy thirteen-year-old boy, so his death took everyone by surprise.

"I don't understand how this can be," Tom said, sounding almost panicked. "How can someone die so young?"

I looked out of the window in my friend's bedroom and watched the sun fade in the early winter evening. There would never be a convenient time to answer such a question.

I was able to make it to the funeral in Beijing, an hour train ride from where I lived in Tianjin. Zhechong Li, or "David," as he'd been known in English class, had not been my student; I had shared Class Seven with another foreign teacher, and David happened to be in his group. But I still wanted to be there for the students whom I had taught and who still had him as a classmate. Getting on the school bus that brought us to the funeral, I looked at the students, David's classmates. Their normally smiling, carefree faces looked down and away, and they said nothing. I wondered what I could possibly offer that would be of any help to them.

We arrived at a gate outside the city and rode down a long driveway through a park with several massive gray buildings. We pulled up to one of them and, as a group, made our way up the stairs into what looked like a large modern temple with pillars. Inside, the students sat down in chairs which lined the waiting room, until we would be told what to do next. In the meantime, teachers were giving each mourner a yellow chrysanthemum from gigantic bouquets. The students busily unraveled the strings of multi-colored paper cranes, boats, and hearts on which they had written their memories and expressions of affections to David. A teacher, watching these preparations, soundlessly wept long unbroken tears. I handed her tissues. Relatives and friends of the family drifted by in pairs and small clumps to enter the room where David's body lay and to pay their respects while we waited our turn.

In the meantime, almost everyone was silent and looked downward. One student made an attempt to talk to me.

"Do you believe in re-. . .something?" She struggled to say the correct word in English.

"Reincarnation?" I asked.

"Yes, I think that's it. When a person is born again."

"I think I know what you mean," I ventured. "I don't think people are born into new people's bodies, but I think the spirit—the part that gives the body life—always stays alive.

She looked thoughtful. "We Chinese believe in reincarnation."

I was curious to ask what she believed, but we were called in to the inner room and had to line up.

When it was our turn, we walked around the casket, which was planted in the center of the room. A large school portrait of the boy surrounded by flowers stood to the side, angled so that we were confronted by his smiling face so alive next to his body. In the casket, well-wishers sending him on his way to the after-life had put stuffed animals, paper, and more flowers into the casket. He was wearing his winter clothes complete with scarf and hat. His pair of gloves had been placed next to his head. It was a strange detail, as if at any moment he might wake up and need to keep his hands warm. It went straight to my heart.

Here we were all crammed into this room, not at all an unusual thing in China. But what was unusual to me was the open expression of emotion without pretense or restraint. I was the only foreigner in a mass of Chinese people, none of whom were trying to restrain or hide deeply felt grief. While that may not seem so odd given the situation, it was a strange contrast to what I had observed in my previous two years in China. On occasions that seemed to call for an open expression of joy, such as a child returning home after months away at university, the reaction was much more subdued than I would have expected. Instead of hugs or words of affection, a parent might give a curt greeting and more often than not, a few words of mild criticism. Sometimes on the street, there might be a brief burst of irritation, but it would dissipate as quickly as it had arisen.

At the other extreme, many people in China seemed to use dramatic emotional displays to manipulate a situation to their advantage. Walking down almost any typical street in China, there would be the almost inevitable witness to the all too common scenario: The Girlfriend and the Boyfriend Having an Argument. Many young Chinese women have a whole cache of melodramatic poses with which to enthrall their boyfriends. They include anything from pouts, whines, and shrug offs to the more attention-getting weeping and kneeling and begging, all of which make for entertaining street theater, as the audience is left wondering if the poor boy in question will actually give in to her demands.

Friends who had bargained for me in the market would show such harsh irritability at some perceived slight of injustice from shop assistants that I would murmur, "It's okay, I can pay that price" just to avoid the ugliness. A few minutes later they would be calmly chattering with me again. They were not truly annoyed—this was just a part of the show, the strategy to win the game. It had little to do with their true emotions.

These strange contradictions all manifested traditional Chinese culture. According to the teachings of Confucius, buttressed by Buddhism, it is good form to glide serenely through one's affairs unruffled by deep emotion of any sort. Pragmatically speaking, openly displaying emotion is a way of showing all your cards and allowing unscrupulous people to take advantage. A genuine outburst of feeling may betray a lack of restraint or self-control which would leave one open to criticism. Therefore, the best face to show the world is one of calm, rational self-restraint.

While not expressing every excessive emotion could be seen as a mature orientation towards life, I often felt a void in all this serenity. At worst, a stoic response to all of life's miseries cuts one off from something vital that helps the blood flow more quickly through one's veins—without it, one becomes almost literally petrified with a heart of stone. I'd seen this response in university students: facing their future with little enthusiasm, their careers having been chosen for them by others, and with little opportunity for exploring their own interests. They seemingly fast-forwarded to middle age, not even bothering with the crisis. At its most extreme, cutting oneself off from showing emotion not only cuts a person off from himself, it also cuts that person off from empathy. Even if one somehow manages to stay in touch with his/her own feelings, how could this person feel sympathy for someone who seemingly had none? Who would want to stay alive for long in a society like this?

Thus far in China I'd seen stoic emotion. I'd seen theatrical emotion. Until now, I often wondered how often I'd seen much genuine emotion. In China, it seemed, there were few occasions when it is appropriate to express true, unvarnished emotion without censure. At this funeral, however, where there was no sensible way to explain this all away, no calm way to accept this fate, I felt a deep pain that actually seemed to approach happiness—or was it relief? This I could relate to. This I could understand. It was a widening of my perspective to be in this room of openly grieving Chinese people. We were all drawn together by this inexplicable tragedy. There was no good reason in any terms, or in any culture, for this young boy to die, and so the only appropriate response, in human terms, was a wordless and open admission of sadness.

David's mother spoke, saying something about "Shangdi," or God, receiving him and then burst into tears, letting them flow. While mourners sobbed openly, Tom and his classmates together recited a poetic speech which Laura, another classmate, had written to express how they would miss him. Tom had roughly translated it for me on the way there on the bus in order to help me understand. It was a piece that asked poignant questions: "I see your pens and paper, but where have you gone?" Several of the students, including Tom, always so practical and eager to do their best in order to make their way in a competitive world, were in tears during the recitation.

The room felt heavy with a helpless sadness and unasked questions which no sensible, practical advice could quell, and so there was compassion. For a few magnificently forlorn moments, the masks were put down.

After putting our flowers on the casket, we formed a line in a semicircle to greet the parents. When it was my turn, the principal explained who I was while I wondered what I could say with my limited language skills. Instead, it was David's father who said, in English, "Thank you so much for coming." Here he was using his language ability to reach out to me in his pain. Then, even more remarkably, his mother, who had never met me before and who had accepted each greeting with a calm dignity, simply gripped me in a tight hug and cried into my neck for a few moments. I wasn't sure if she would ever let go and I'll never know what opened that dam for her in that moment, but it somehow didn't matter. Despite the strange public nature of it, we were united in our needs—mine to comfort and hers to be comforted—and also in our common need for a belief in an afterlife. The pause, which seemed to hold for an eternity, was soon over with the principal tapping my shoulder, quietly signaling the time for exit.

6

What Shall I Call You?

by Pamela Holt

O N THE FIRST DAY of every class, I ask my students to fill out a Get-to-Know-You sheet with their names, student numbers, home-towns and an icebreaker question like "What is your favorite thing to do on the weekend?" One of my goals is to learn all of their names. I ask for their names in Chinese, in pinyin romanization complete with tones, and in English if they have one. Then I take pictures of the students as they hold up cards with their names written on them. During my first year in China I learned that some students do not like to take English names. Their Chinese names are their real names, so they want their teachers to use them. But I have also had students say none of their other teachers, even in elementary school, ever knew their names. Learning their names, and the meanings of their names, is one way I can learn who they really are and appreciate them as individuals.

Names make a great topic of conversation for visiting hours: Why parents chose the name they chose, or What they hope for their son or daughter as a result. The meanings of names are much clearer in Chinese than in English because they are composed of ordinary Chinese words, not adapted from Greek, Norwegian, or French. Many names include *hua*, which stands for China, or *hong,* which means "red." The East is Red, Mao said. "East" is another common character. I once taught a group of deans and vice deans who were embarrassed by the political names some of them had been given in the early years of the People's Republic of China—"The East is Rising," "Eternal Soldier." Today, many students' names mean "strong," "beautiful," or "treasure." One of my current students' names is derived from a common phrase meaning "Develop China."

Westerners have a limited number of given names, but a wide variety of surnames, while Chinese have a limited number of surnames ("the people" are commonly referred to as "Old Hundred Names"), but a wide variety of given names. But when I have four girls named Ting Ting out of 150 students, I wonder why that name became so popular twenty years ago. In three cases, the characters mean "graceful," but the fourth Ting Ting, oddly enough, means "imperial court." Since the pronunciation is the same, I am just thankful they have different surnames. Double names like Ting Ting, Qian Qian ("q" is pronounced "ch"), and Yan Yan are quite common, especially for girls. My (male) class leader this term is called Kai Kai ("triumphant"), but his friends just call him Kai. He seems embarrassed by the double name. Some names are clearly for boys and others for girls. But I also have four students with the given name Lei (pronounced like a Hawaiian lei), which means "open and upright." Three are boys, one is a girl. Again I am thankful they have different family names, as it would be awkward to have a male and a female student with the exact same name in the same class.

I have learned many of the most common names and each year recognize more, but many names are unusual. Parents or grandparents go to the dictionary to find words with good meanings and sometimes choose obscure words. Some of my students have even said their names changed in elementary school because the official record was different from their parents' intention. A clerk wrote the wrong character on the form, but the mistake was only discovered when the child registered for school and it was too late to change it. It is easy to make such a mistake since so many characters have the same pronunciation.

For non-Chinese speakers, Chinese names are just random sounds. For Chinese speakers, the same is true of typical Western names. Chinese Christians complain that it is hard to remember Biblical names because the characters don't mean anything. Zedekiah doesn't mean anything to me either unless I look up the Hebrew. Multicultural societies must be more tolerant of names composed of unfamiliar combinations of sounds. But in any culture, people don't always think of the meaning of a name when they use it as a name. One of my childhood friends was a girl named Sweetie. Mr. Shofner, our ninth-grade biology teacher, was uncomfortable calling one of his students Sweetie, but she protested "It's my name!" Eventually he got used to it. Similarly, my students in China call one another "Handsome and Cultured" or "Elegant Beauty" without any embarrassment. It's their name.

My own Chinese name was given to me by my first Chinese teacher, an immigrant from Shanghai who taught me some basic Chinese while I was in graduate school in California. She spent a lot of time choosing a name with the right meaning and the right sound. Each syllable is related to my English name, but also has its own significance. My surname Holt was transliterated to He (pronounced "Huh?"), but she pointed out that the character is pronounced Ho in the south of China, which is closer to Holt. "He" basically means "what" and is a fairly common surname. My given names (Pamela Diane) were represented with Pei Dan (pronounced approximately "Pay Don"). The words mean "admire" and "red," but also "to wear a pin" and "to be loyal." My teacher considered the deeper meaning to be "to have a loyal heart," particularly in my relationship to God. It is a name to live up to. Once, when I told my name to a Chinese friend, I used the wrong tones and called myself "Admirable Egg," so she suggested I change it to something easier to say. The next time I saw my teacher she drilled me repeatedly on my pronunciation. Now I get compliments on what I am told is a very traditional Chinese name.

It is useful to have a name others can remember. Transliterating non-Chinese names into Chinese produces long strings of syllables that don't mean anything. When I arrived in China, I was given the name Pa Mei La He Le Te (in pinyin "e" is said "uh") – a transliteration of Pamela Holt into a syllable-based language with no final consonants except "n" and "ng." I can't write it, and nobody can remember it. He Pei Dan is easy for people to remember, easy to write, and also widely enough known that even mail sent to 何佩丹 at Shandong University is delivered. I am often called Teacher He around campus.

Titles like "Teacher" are important in China. Many people are called by their title along with their surname, such as President Zhan or Dean Gao. In my province, people will address strangers as "Teacher." Sometimes teachers from other provinces are surprised and ask, "How did they know I'm a teacher?" Such courtesy is much more important in China than in the U.S. It is also polite to add "Xiao" (meaning "little") or "Lao" (literally "old" but maybe better translated "elder") to a surname, depending on whether the speaker is older or younger than the person spoken to or has a higher or lower social position. I realized at the end of my first year of teaching that I had been informally calling some of my students by their Chinese given names. If their name had three characters, I would only use the last two (since Chinese surnames are listed first). It was easier for me to remember two syllables instead of three, but I decided it was arrogant for me to assume I could use their given names without permission. After all, I asked them to call me Dr. Holt, so perhaps I should return the courtesy by using their full name. So I started asking the students to tell me what they want me to call them. They often choose their full name, but sometimes they choose an English name or a nickname like Xiao Nan or Xiao Xu. None have yet asked me to use Lao, nor do they use Lao with me. One student did ask me to call him Dr. Zhang, but I refused until he had earned his Ph.D.

When Chinese students choose English names, the results can be unconventional. But unusual names have advantages. It is difficult to forget Cuckoo and Morphine, even if they change their names later to Kevin and Stephen. Some students go to the dictionary and just translate their Chinese name, like "Stone," " Bright," or "Crystal." But what if one's name means "world peace"? Other times they choose English names that sound like their Chinese names. I can't fault Li Li for deciding to be called Lily, even if she is the fifteenth Lily I have taught. Sometimes the English equivalent is obvious. When we met a boy named Wang Xin Tian at church, I spontaneously christened him Washington ("x" is pronounced "hs"). And I suggested Jinglin call himself Julian, when Jobless was the closest thing he could find on his own. The students prefer names with obvious meanings, so Sunny and Spring are popular. And they always want to know what the name means. Sometimes they name themselves after famous people. Several years ago a student wanted to be called Kobe, but I hadn't heard of Kobe Bryant yet and spelled it Coby. The boys love basketball, and want to emulate NBA stars like Michael Jordan. Because of the name order difference, they usually call themselves Jordan, not Michael.

Name order is decidedly confusing. The students are well aware of the difference in Western name order, so sometimes they will write their pinyin names in Western order to "help" me. It is nearly impossible for a Westerner to decide which name is the surname, unless the surname is in all capitals. Take my former student Zhou Yang for example. Zhou and Yang are both possible surnames. Is she Yang ZHOU or Zhou YANG? Her name was derived by combining her father's and mother's surnames. Even a Chinese person reading the characters would not know which was which.

Knowing the students' names probably encourages them to come to class, but I don't want them to think I learn their names only so that I can keep track of their attendance. I want to remember my student's names because it means so much to them to be known. In a society with so many people with the same name, and with so many people vying for the same position, being known by name is greatly significant. Calling them by name is one way to show I care about them. The only difficulty is that after the semester is over, I promptly forget all the names I worked so hard to learn. As I get older and have met more Jings and Juns, Jennys and Jordans, I find them more difficult to memorize and easier to forget. But God knows their names. And He does not forget.

7

Lost and Found in Yunnan

by Lindsey Paulick

I HAD FEWER THAN four days left to decide how I would spend my first Chinese holiday, and things weren't looking promising. While I liked the idea of celebrating the National Holiday commemorating the first official day of Communism (not ideologically, but at least in the spirit of experiencing Chinese culture to its fullest), I had only recently arrived in the small town of Baoding and had not yet made a close enough friend with whom I could travel. Besides, it was too last minute to plan a trip of any significance.

Or so I thought. Turns out, China is a land where travel plans, teaching schedules, and in fact most business is conducted "last minute." On my second-hand cell-phone, three days before our first day of vacation, I received a text message (the communication method of choice for most young people in China due to the next-to-nothing cost and ability to compose messages silently under desks in the back or front of class). It was from a Chinese girl I had met the week before at a dinner with some other foreigners. Celia, (whose Chinese name is Niu Jin Hui, which took me the entire week to memorize) is an ex-English teacher from Baoding whose husband played basketball with some of my fellow foreign teachers. Celia had already decided that I was to be her travel partner. After convincing me it was possible to book a trip with such late notice and taking several wild and life-threatening scooter rides across town to various travel agents, we decided on a destination. It was the place of her childhood dreams and one that I had recently heard was the most ideal vacation spot in China: Yunnan, the Land of Eternal Spring.

Though there are so many things to do in Yunnan Province, we decided the eight-day trip would be a little tough on our budgets and time schedules, so we settled for a five-day four-night tour of Yunnan, which included flights, room, board, travel, and most entry fees. 3,500 yuan seemed like a pretty good deal for all this, especially relative to travel costs in the States, and besides, this was the reason I had worked and saved money all summer. Even though it cost me an extra 500 yuan for being a foreigner (I'm still not exactly sure what this fee covered—extra paper work? Extra security expenses for a suspicious foreigner?) and I was going to be the only non-Chinese person on the tour, we decided to go for it. Three days later, we were on a three-hour flight to Kunming, the capital of Yunnan.

Since it was Celia's first time on a plane, we were thankful for the uneventful flight. We arrived at our hotel past midnight and were up with the rest of the tour group by six a.m. There were two things I immediately noticed as we made our way out to the tour bus with our luggage, two minutes before the scheduled departure time. First, we were late. Yes, we were two minutes early, but by Chinese tour group standards, we were at least ten minutes late. I realized this was going to be a challenge for me the rest of the trip as I boarded the bus with twenty-eight sets of eyes fixed on me. I'm pretty sure it wasn't just because I was the only foreigner.

The other thing that might have had something to do with the stares was the shocking scene I had just created as I half rolled, half dragged my medium-sized duffle bag which was at least three times the size of any other bag or suitcase on the trip, onto the bus. Never mind that the travel agent told me I could pack as much as I wanted or needed. While I had planned for all sorts of inclement weather—it *could* still rain in the Land of Eternal Spring—everyone else in the group had managed to pack their five-day trip into small backpacks and suitcases the size of shoeboxes. I kicked myself for being such a conspicuous American tourist as I found my seat next to Celia. (By the way, I did learn from this experience. When my sister came to visit two months later, we took a four-day trip to Shanghai and fit everything into our school backpacks. Apparently you really can wear the same shirt two days in a row and you only *need* one pair of shoes. Who knew?)

While I was ready to fall right back to sleep as soon as my head hit the back of the surprisingly comfortable reclining tour bus seat, my travel companion had other plans. She, as was the case with most of my Chinese friends, wanted to improve her English as much as possible while she had the opportunity. On the six-hour drive out of Kunming through minority group villages nestled in rolling green hills and the most vibrant blue sky I had seen since leaving the States, she attempted to translate the stories and history lessons that our hard-working tour guide relayed over the screechy loud speaker for the entire trip, stopping only when the bus stopped for breaks along the sides of the highways. I appreciated her effort to keep me informed on the local culture, but listening and trying to translate broken English into something comprehensible for hours at a time could be the cure for any insomniac. A bathroom break and caffeinated soda were just what I needed.

The bathroom breaks, however, brought an unanticipated source of stress to this adventure. Having been in China for only around six weeks at this point, I was still in the honeymoon stage, almost believing that culture shock was for the weak and feeble-minded. This trip did its part in humbling that view right out of me, starting as soon as I walked into the gas station bathroom and began frantically and fruitlessly looking around for the squatty-potty stalls that actually had doors. Before this, I had been to China and other parts of the world that had the toilets where you have to squat down instead of the Western ones where you sit—I can absolutely handle that. Bringing my own toilet paper and hand sanitizer? No problem. Going out in the woods on a camping trip? Easy. But having a group of curious old Chinese women stare shamelessly at you while you try to discreetly do your business? This was beyond my comfort zone. The first two attempts at relieving myself were entirely unsuccessful. It wasn't until our third pit stop at an out-of-the-way restaurant when I snuck out in the middle of lunch to an empty bathroom that I was finally able to go. How was I going to survive an entire week of this?

The incredible panoramas of wide green valleys dotted with rooftops colored in yellow corn and bright red peppers took my mind off of my predicament. Our next stop was the town of Dali, the ancient capital city of the Bai and Nanzhou kingdoms and so famous for the marble it produces that "Dali-stone" is the literal Chinese translation of the word "marble." It is now a major tourist hotspot and attracts thousands of tourists every year, both foreign and Chinese. While we made our way through Yunnan, I surveyed the people in my tour group and wondered how I was to befriend any of them. So far, no one (besides Celia) had even attempted to speak English with me, and my Mandarin was still rudimentary at best. Celia gave me lessons on our drive. We started with how to tell people about my family. "I have a twin sister. My dad is a businessman." My first attempts at using my new phrases were met with blank stares and uncomfortable silences. This was not going as planned. A major breakthrough came at one of our tourist destinations when a young girl from our group (I would've guessed fifteen—come to find out later she's older than me and in her late twenties) ran up to me out of nowhere, put a flower lei on my head, and turned me towards her husband who snapped a picture. Apparently, this ambush had been in the works for awhile, ever since my new friend, named Wu Ying, realized there was a foreigner in the tour group.

Over the next couple of days, as her English improved—most young Chinese people have a solid foundation of English vocabulary from their school days but it gets buried when not used regularly—she shyly explained that she was on her honeymoon and that her one wish for the trip was to meet a foreigner. Being from a wealthy but small town, she had never before had the opportunity to actually talk to a foreigner. Since I also wanted to make new friends, we quickly hit it off, even though our conversation soon dried up after we discussed our families, their jobs, and the weather. She constantly insisted on buying me local snacks and novelty items which I used to fill the remaining space in my gigantic suitcase. At one stop, there was a local minority group game that looked something like basketball. I was surprised to discover that Wu Ying actually had some basketball skills, which she easily adapted to this game, making shot after shot into the three-sided hoop. She was easily the most athletic Chinese girl I had ever met, which was a pleasant surprise. Most Chinese girls I have encountered are very sweet and hospitable, but we have a hard time finding things in common. I am constantly reassuring them that it is normal for girls to play soccer in America and explaining why I don't like to go shopping if I can avoid it. Wu Ying also had a surprising understanding and sensitivity towards American culture which, through Celia's translation, she explained was from her parents. She said her father and mother always encouraged her to be strong and independent, to follow her dreams, and to not feel burdened to take care of them as they aged. The longer I was in China, the more I realized how exceedingly rare that was. It was nice to experience a friendship, however brief, where both sides were trying equally hard to understand and accommodate the other's culture.

Cultural experiences were certainly not lacking during this five-day tour. We must have made more than thirty stops at local restaurants, cultural heritage museums and gardens, temples, pagodas, waterfalls, bridges, lakes, late-night karaoke, and the always-interesting Chinese traditional medicine shops. We saw acrobats perform in the circus and elephants walk over a line of two dozen eager tourists. We explored the streets of old town Lijiang, joined in with local ethnic minority group youth dancing around a bonfire at night, and ate crustaceans from the village lakes.

After a few solid days of this, I was ready for some alone time. I found my opportunity at the Stone Forest, a major tourist attraction outside Kunming where thousands come each day to admire the giant slabs of granite rock jutting up like the sequoias in the California state parks. While most of the group followed our tour guide, who was explaining the scientific and cultural history of the area, I decided to make my escape. Knowing by now that Chinese people aren't interested in letting anyone, let alone foreigners like me, do anything alone, I knew I'd have to be sneaky. So that she wouldn't worry, I told Celia, who by now had given up trying to translate anything but pertinent information from the tour guide—how long till we arrive, when's the next bathroom break— that I was going to go explore. I promised to be very careful and to take my cell phone, plenty of water, sun block, and mosquito repellent. And I'd be back in forty-five minutes.

Laughing to myself about how much my Chinese friends needlessly worried about me, I set off, aiming to get as far away from groups of people as possible in the limited amount of time I had. It wasn't too hard to do either, since most groups stayed within a half-mile of the entrance. Soon I was navigating the deep crevasses and narrow staircases on my own, relishing the silence and space. After taking some self-portraits and finishing off my water, I decided I should start heading back. Although I have been known to have a pretty inaccurate sense of direction, I have noticed it improving in the last few years, so I decided it was reliable enough to get me back in the general direction from where I had come. I found the staircase that had led me out to the meadow and calculated my ETA to be at least ten minutes early. I was fine.

But I soon realized that I had recognized the staircases and passageways because they all looked exactly the same! I could still sense the general direction I needed to go, but I couldn't figure out how to get there. Unable to say the name of the meeting spot in Chinese, I couldn't ask for directions, and of course, my cell phone wasn't getting any reception. By the time I meandered my way through the maze of stairways and to the top of the forest so I could look out and find my way, I was ten minutes later than the time we had agreed upon. This would not have been a big deal, except that this was China and they had probably already sent out a search party. When I finally found my way, the entire tour group was sitting on the curb waiting for me. When they saw me jogging up, half of them ran over to welcome me back while the rest started calling the tour guide and his helpers to call off the search. While I apologized for keeping them all waiting and worrying, an older lady whom I had tried to befriend on the first day came up and grabbed my arm. Uh oh, I was in for it. Still holding on to my arm, she fished through her purse and found a small green bottle from which she took some ointment and started digging her nail into and slapping my arm. Startled, I laughed when I realized she had noticed me itching the fresh mosquito bites on my arm and wanted to alleviate the inflammation. She smiled and laughed with me as she gave a big hug as if to say "We're so glad you're safe!" I felt like a long-lost daughter coming home, though I wasn't able to say more than two sentences to this lady or her family during the entire trip.

Exhausted after a long day in the sun, Celia and I settled into our last hotel of the trip, an unusually modern and clean three-star hotel in the heart of Kunming. I checked out the bathroom and was pleasantly surprised to see that the shower had a door to separate it from the sink and toilet, as well as a sign above the toilet. Throughout the trip I had been trying to hold in chuckles as I read signs warning English speakers in "Chinglish" (a literal and often unintentionally humorous translation of Chinese into English by Chinese speakers) to "Slip and Fall Down Carefully" and encouraging you to watch your step on the grass with "Your Careful Step Keeps Tiny Grass Invariably Green." While still trying to be sensitive to Celia, I couldn't help laughing at this sign above the toilet with a picture of a stick-man slipping with the words "Beware of Landslide!" printed above it. As humorous as it was, this kind of sign was now a constant reminder to me of how much my Chinese hosts wanted to care for and protect me.

As culture shock wore off during the following months of teaching, I was more and more able to appreciate and learn from the hospitality and genuine care displayed by the many friends I met throughout my stay. Though I struggled with culture shock during this short vacation, I also had the opportunity to see Chinese culture at its finest and made memories and friendships that will last a lifetime.

8

Searching for Lu Xun

by Robert Moore

THE FIRST TIME I ever tried reading Lu Xun was during a six-week stint teaching at Peking University. I had a copy of *The True Story of Ah Q* in English that a friend had given me, so one day during my lunch break I went to a little place that specialized in Beijing meat pies (hard to explain, good to eat) and started reading.

It was a masterpiece of modern Chinese literature, so I had heard.

It was a part of the Chinese canon.

Lu Xun was a master.

I read about ten pages, frowned, turned the book over to look at the glowing comments, went back to the text, frowned, and repeated the process.

"If this is a part of the canon," I thought, "then Chinese readers must have a pretty thin time of it."

The character of Ah Q came across like a clown—and not a particularly intelligent clown. You know, the guy in high school who isn't a great athlete, isn't cool, isn't good-looking, and so takes refuge in humor? Only he isn't all that funny, either? That's Ah Q in the English translation—pathetic, and in many cases, because of the differences in cultures, bizarre. I couldn't for the life of me figure out one of the opening sequences, where Ah Q is debating with someone about his family background. It was virtually incomprehensible. And inane. Without any appropriate context, it's like encountering Faulkner for the first time through the scene in *As I Lay Dying* where Vardaman decides his dead mother is a fish. So I shrugged, set down *Ah Q*, which I'd managed to grease up nicely by handling it with the same fingers I'd used to eat my lunch, and read something else.

I didn't read Lu Xun again until some years later. By that time I was able to read him in Chinese. You probably know what I'm going to say next, so I'll just go ahead and say it—it's a completely different experience in the original language. I know that's a fairly beaten-to-death cliché, but it's true nonetheless. I honestly don't think it's possible to translate Lu Xun into English, for the same reason that I don't think it's possible to translate P.G. Wodehouse or John Steinbeck into Chinese, namely, that Lu Xun, like Wodehouse and Steinbeck, is a master of local dialect. One of the complaints against writers like John Steinbeck is that his characters sound like uneducated hicks. But that's the way such people talk.

I'll never forget my first experience plowing through a dialogue between Ah Q and a beggar. The local argot was so perfectly done that I laughed out loud in the middle of the coffee shop. I had heard cab drivers and fruit vendors in Beijing and Tianjin speaking exactly the same way. Even Ah Q's reasoning was familiar. No matter what the situation, he looks for the practical gain, even on the eve of revolution in a scene which for me is one of the greatest dark comedic demonstrations ever, where he spends the night wondering, not if he will live or die, but which of his neighbors will be killed first and which of their grieving widows would be worth seducing. Macabre, yes, but if you ever get a chance to read the scene in Chinese, you'll laugh just as I did.

Naturally, because I was so excited about Lu Xun's writing, I wanted other people to share in the experience. I tried to engage my students many times in discussions about him. It never worked. They just stared blankly or shuffled uncomfortably in their seats when I asked them for their impressions. (Granted, they do this when I ask them just about everything else, too, from "Do you think it's more important to be rich or happy?" to "IS there a holiday on Monday?") The immediate response I got, when I mentioned having read Lu Xun in Chinese, was shock.

"But he's so difficult to understand!"

"Even we Chinese don't understand him very well!"

This mystified me at first. And frustrated me. One semester I decided to form a literature discussion group where the students could discuss in Chinese, believing this would make them comfortable enough to open up. I chose as our focus the question "If China were to have a fixed literary canon, who would be in it?" They threw themselves into the question, and for several weeks we had spirited discussions about whether or not to include Zhu Ziqing ("His essays aren't original!" "I don't care! He's still brilliant!") or whether or not Mao Zedong was actually a good poet. That particular question split the group in half for a week or two until we added a member who could break the tie. If I remember correctly, the tie-breaker didn't like the Chairman's poetry.

One week I suggested, after we had finished creating a Chinese canon, that we select a writer and a representative work to read and discuss.

My suggestion was met with a stony silence.

One student frowned and asked, "But who will tell us the meaning of the book?"

He meant that since there was no official teacher present, there was no recognized expert among us.

Thinking I was forging into new and welcome territory, I said brightly, "Well, if we all read the book together and share our thoughts and feelings, then I think we'll gain a very good understanding."

More silence.

I figured that at least the literature major in our group would be excited. But she didn't seem any more responsive than anyone else. It mystified me. It truly did. Why would intelligent Chinese people not want to personally engage the great minds of their culture?

Why, indeed? I was aware, very much so, of the nature of Chinese education, especially of the tendency to lecture rather than engage. Students in middle and high school are given countless classic texts to read. But they are never encouraged to think about the meaning for themselves. The teacher gives the approved interpretation, then moves on. The students are told what their opinion should be.

I even encountered this when one of my students offered to teach me about Tang Dynasty poetry. The time-honored way to read poetry in the West is to approach the text slowly, cautiously, and from different angles. We are taught to bring our memories, our personal inclinations, and our biases into the experience, and then allow the poem to become something unique to ourselves.

With my friend it was different. We read a poem in Chinese. Then he told me what it meant.

"This character means 'Mongolian grassland.'"

"This one refers to an ancient temple."

There could be no debate about the accuracy of his interpretation. His teacher had taught him this particular meaning, and that's what it was. Where I was trying to find some personal handle on the poem, he was seeking to impart an "accurate" rendering. In group-oriented China, there is no room in the average Chinese classroom for personal engagement with a text. I knew all that when I began getting frustrated with my students. But knowing something about a foreign culture doesn't generally result in peace of mind. I know there isn't a single academic department on my campus which will make a plan more than one week in advance, and I can even tell you why, but it still makes me want to beat my head against a wall.

Plus, the issue was deeper than pedagogy. Some years before this, before I had begun studying Chinese literature, I met up with a Chinese friend in Dalian. One night we started talking about literature. A compilation of Lu Xun's essays was sitting on a rickety table near one of the beds, and in answer to my query, both my friend and his roommate immediately became very serious.

"If you want to understand anything about modern China," said my friend, "you must read Lu Xun."

I've since heard this multiple times from other students. A colleague of mine at Tianjin University had his students write a short paper on Lu Xun, and most of them referred to him as "China's greatest writer" without qualification, as though it were a foregone conclusion, something everyone knew as instinctively as the existence of gravity.

But while I have been told many times I should study Lu Xun, my students and friends generally smile and shake their heads when I suggest the same for them. The belief is simply that a person can't understand Lu Xun or at least can't *fully* understand him. It's an attitude with roots as far back as Confucius—and probably before him. It can be summarized simply: the master is the master, and the student is the student. If a student completely understands everything the master says, he or she is on the same level as the master. The idea that someone could ever be on the same level as Lu Xun is laughable—therefore no one will ever understand him.

This is not the kind of inquiry Confucius or his followers were getting at, but this is the way intellectual thought is understood in many places. Certainly it works this way in graduate study in China, at least in the sciences. I have had many discussions with my students, few of whom are in the liberal arts, about their research. The average Chinese graduate student does not choose a research project—his project is chosen by the professor and is usually a part of the professor's own research. The student is not encouraged to challenge the professor's research, even if it appears deeply flawed, but is expected simply to work hard. Later on, when that student is a professor, then he or she can question at will. But in the short term, the professor is the professor, and the student the student. When I mention to my students that a good professor in America (not every professor, of course, but a good one) welcomes challenges from students, provided they have good reasons for disagreeing, my students smile and shake their heads. "We would never do that here," they always remark.

What's intriguing in all of this is that while most Chinese people I've met are familiar with Lu Xun the political revolutionary, few seem to have much taste for his writings. They're aware of his historical impact, but almost oblivious to his stylistic influence. In many ways, Lu Xun was China's Pushkin—a writer who began using his nation's colloquial language to create high art. In order to do this, of course, he had to abandon many of the established classical forms. In China, even today, students are taught the language using the same classical forms that Lu Xun avoided. Children in Chinese elementary schools are required to memorize and recite ancient poems. They aren't expected to understand them, but merely to learn the characters and rhythms. (Imagine the horrors an elementary school teacher would go through in America if every student had to recite Shakespearean sonnets.) In a second-grade reader that I used when first learning Chinese, there were multiple poems from the Tang Dynasty poets Du Fu and Li Bai, both considered to be masters of the form in China. From a young age, then, Chinese students become accustomed to a certain standard when it comes to poetry. Poems must have a fixed rhythm and rhyme scheme. They must be symmetrical on the page. They must sound and feel a certain way. As a result, I have yet to meet a single Chinese person who enjoys reading contemporary Chinese poetry as much as classical poetry.

Lu Xun, by comparison, is different. His style doesn't adhere to any of the established classical forms. Too, because he was also a supporter of early revolutionary movements and wrote pointed and often scathing social satire, he is often cast as a political figure more than a writer.

"Why is Lu Xun so great?" I often asked my students.

"Because he taught the Chinese people how to revolt," they invariably answered.

Lu Xun had something to say—he was trying to teach. Each of his writings has a clear revolutionary message, usually communicated through his profound understanding of Chinese society. His writing must be understood in this way. Enjoying *The True Story of Ah Q* simply because it's funny or *Wild Grass* simply because of its bizarre and beautiful dreamscapes is absurd without understanding Lu Xun's "message." It would be like reading *The Communist Manifesto* as a piece of interesting prose rather than as a revolutionary document.

My neighbor Peter and I were once discussing whether or not Lu Xun could be considered a national writer, a sort of Pushkin or Shakespeare. I maintained then that he wasn't, but now I'm not so sure. It's a complicated question. I believe he embodies the things many Chinese people feel but are afraid to let rise to the surface. Although he was a revolutionary, he was deeply pessimistic and never believed the revolution would succeed. He fought because he believed there was no other option. While most of my students seem to be optimistic about modern China, there is a strong undercurrent of fear and foreboding that no one wants to express. This year, for example, it is estimated that almost one-third of all graduating college students in China will be unemployed. These same students have been raised to see China's development optimistically, and yet now that they are faced with the stark realities of a bloated job market, they have begun to consciously or unconsciously echo Lu Xun's equally stark observations about the failings in his own society. He was and is a writer who put the spirit of the Chinese people on the page, even when that spirit differed from the dominant propaganda of the day.

Although he was supportive of many socialist aims, Lu Xun never officially joined the Communist Party, not even in the Party's glory days. He wrote dark, brooding prose that criticized the common people as much as their leaders. He also read and studied mostly Western works, seeking in modern French and Russian literature the tools with which to create a modern Chinese literature.

He was and is a difficult writer to label—a national writer who criticized his nation, a stylist whose style is still impossible to emulate, a revolutionary who didn't believe the revolution would succeed, a very Chinese writer who used un-Chinese forms. How does a good Chinese student approach a figure like this?

Perhaps a better question would be this: When will China be ready for Lu Xun? The popular perception of modern China in the dominant Chinese media—and amongst at least a large percentage of the population—is that it is a country with a fixed course, an ancient power which is poised to become a power again. Things are all on the rise. It's as though China's success is destiny.

With this perception, there isn't much room for Lu Xun. There's room for Lu Xun the socialist revolutionary, the man who helped propel China to retake its historical pride. But there isn't room for Lu Xun the conflicted, brilliant artist. Those of my students and friends who do enjoy Lu Xun are themselves conflicted about the state of their country. They enjoy the new economic prosperity, but wonder where their culture is going. They have learned to enjoy his writings, not as propaganda, but to identify with his world of images and scenes.

Ultimately, appreciating a writer as complex and individual as Lu Xun isn't a matter of correct interpretation, but of a willingness to accept paradox and ambiguity in a culture. The trouble for any Chinese student when dealing with Lu Xun is the same as that encountered in the job market, in the classroom, and sometimes in the home—the officially accepted conclusions don't fit. Lu Xun wrote during a time when Chinese scholars and ordinary people alike were looking for something new. Because there were few precedents in Chinese history to guide them, they had to engage other writings and ideas on a personal level. This led not only to new forms of Chinese writing, but to new ideas and new problems. Appreciating the complexity of this search is not a purely social endeavor, but a personal one as well, just as it was for the writers themselves. And so long as Lu Xun is confined to the sterile summaries of a classroom, he will never be the national writer China needs, but only the one it expects.

9

Lessons for the Teacher

by Daniel Jaime

THE STUDENTS I TEACH in China vary from freshmen to graduate levels. Every day when I walk into a classroom a transformation takes place. I become a student in the presence of sixty to seventy teachers. To some this might seem a bit strange, but indeed I have learned as much or more from my students as they from me.

During a class discussion about the roles of fathers and mothers in Chinese families, one student talked about how his father washed dishes and clothes in order to help his mother with housework. Most of his male classmates found this hard to believe. At the time, I also found it hard to believe, as my limited knowledge of Chinese culture told me the husband is the breadwinner and ruler of the household. Washing dishes and clothes for a Chinese man was out of the question. I was wrong.

My personal journal is full of many similar entries. Every page is an education gleaned from the minds of my young teachers, bringing me face to face with one of the world's most fascinating cultures.

LESSONS ABOUT FAMILY

For thousands of years in China, generations of families have lived under one roof. The same holds true today. Herein lies the extended Chinese family, or "Big Family," as referred to by one of my students. China has a one-child policy, and most students from the city are only children. However, it is not uncommon to hear students from the rural areas talk about large families of four or five children.

The Chinese believe the family helps shape the way one sees and interacts with the world. Parents discipline and teach children the value of responsibility and of respect for family and elders. Grandparents often care for a grandchild during the day because fathers and mothers work. I remember seeing a grandfather sitting at a small table next to his grandson, seven or eight years old. The boy was looking at a book and the grandfather, pointing to the words with his finger, was teaching him. It was a precious sight. I could tell the grandfather had a great interest in teaching his grandson. Whenever the boy's attention wavered, he would tenderly move his grandson's head back to the book. I have no doubt that when this little boy matures he will remember these precious times with his grandfather.

My students' comments about family are touching, but I also have learned about the pressures some feel in fulfilling their obligations to their families.

Student Comments

Nothing could make me happier than being with my parents. They played an important role in my life. I remember my childhood. My parents were patient, disciplined me, and let me do whatever I wanted. I was not a spoiled girl.

I have seen Chinese couples with a "spoiled" child—their patience is impeccable, but there is eventually a break in their tolerance.

Family is a small part of society, but when valued and in harmony becomes the foundation of society. Families stay together through the difficult and happy times. One gathers his strength from family and it is important to forgive when tension arises amongst members.

This student also told me he is grateful for all his parents have done for him. Without their love, there is no family.

Such profound statements are not questioned when it comes to the values held in Chinese society about family. When this student graduates, he wants to get a good job and buy a house for his parents.

Family is a safe harbor; you can come to it during troubled times. You can feel free to cry, laugh, show anger and be loved. I feel free when I am with family and I can be myself where people understand me. My family is important.

The family values taught to this student are deep-rooted. It is my belief they will be passed on to another generation.

> *When I first met the English word "family," my teacher told us that is the abbreviation for "Father and Mother, I love you." I thought it is just a coincidence for the moment. Later and now, I think it is true. In my opinion, all the members of the family should love others and be loved. Parents are the people who bring you to the world; they give all their love to you. You should respect and love them all your life. Children are the hope and future of our world. Parents should love, encourage, and teach them to learn to be grateful and to be a useful person to the whole society.*

F.A.M.I.L.Y. – noted in my journal.

> *We should be full of gratefulness and let the members of our family know we love them. Home is the place where we can laugh or cry loudly, where everyone puts his or her heart into loving and caring for you. It is the place where we can be wrong and no one will criticize you.*

The word "acceptance" comes to mind when I read these students' comments. It is no wonder many of my students miss home during school and look forward to holidays with family.

Consider this next comment and note how some traditional practices bring about pressure. Some students told me the pressure comes from current changes taking place in China, which are shaking the foundational structure of traditional Chinese families.

> *To me, family is the more important than anything else. I want to try to do my best to keep my family harmonious and healthy. I was born to take responsibility for taking care of the old and young in the family. If I do not, my conscience will punish me. It is immoral to refuse to take care of your family.*

Are the student's comments more out of social conditioning or from a respectful, willing heart? Is it possible her parents have imposed this conviction upon her? Nevertheless, she is willing to do what it takes to care for the family. She and her husband may someday be caring for four sets of grandparents and two sets of parents.

One student was confused about an article she had read about young married couples not wanting to live with parents and share the burden of caring for them when they get older. I still remember the look on her face. The article shattered her cultural upbringing.

I appreciate my students' comments on the importance of family. Some are determined to uphold family obligations while others are trying to cope with the changes affecting them. Students' comments about their family being a safe harbor where they can come during troubled times is my reminder to those who are not fulfilling family obligations.

THE IMPORTANCE OF EDUCATION

Three words describe the system of education endured by my students prior to entering university—study, memorization, and tests. Entrance exam scores determine advancement through the academic world. These entrance exams are for middle school, high school, and college. The caliber of school to which a student is admitted can be important. One student told me the college entrance exam literally holds one's future in its hands. It is true. Unfortunately, some students are not accepted at any university.

The group-orientation of Chinese society has presented some challenges in the classroom, especially for me. In a Chinese classroom, students are hindered from most forms of self-expression—asking questions, participating in discussions, or engaging in arguments. Traditional thinking is that a quiet student learns more and is more respectful than one who speaks up. Because of traditional classroom conduct, the idiom, "If a single bird sticks out his head from the flock, it will be shot," presents a challenge in a foreign English teacher's classroom. Singling oneself out from the group is also considered taking away from the teacher's lesson—a sign of disrespect towards the teacher. Therefore, as a foreign teacher, I have struggled with getting students to speak up in class. I am asking them to act counter to their culture and upbringing.

How have I handled this? Honestly, it has been quite a struggle. Then an American couple with eight years of teaching experience in China taught me to tell students: "This is an American classroom; leave your 'face' outside the door. Do not be afraid to make mistakes or worry about what your classmates will think of you. We learn from our mistakes." With these encouraging words, students have expressed their opinions on many issues, especially those of their particular interest. As the semester wore on, many birds from within the flock began to stick out their heads.

Student Comments

> *Education is of great significance to people. From education, we can improve any qualities and have fun. We can also broaden our minds and express some opinions on certain things.*

As a teacher, I feel good about this comment, especially the latter part, having to do with expressing one's opinion. I want my students to feel confident and comfortable in expressing their opinions.

> *To be a civil person, education is indispensable. If one's education is good, one will be and have a dignified life. Education is making "LIFE." Besides, education gives you a good eye to judge right or wrong.*

"Education is making LIFE." No question about how important education is for this student.

> *Education is one of the most critical parts in a country. To a certain extent, the better the education a country has, the more prosperous the country will be. Because if children accepted a good education, they would be more qualified for their jobs and they would contribute a lot for their country. Then the country would not remain backward.*

The love for the motherland is evident. Earning a degree will help this student bring about a better China by becoming a well-educated citizen for society and helping with the advancement of China.

> *In China, as for education, parents always spare no effort to ensure their children have a good education. Parents place their hope on the children and help them choose the major when they are admitted to a university. Sometimes they may object to the choice of their child if they do not think the major has broad prospects. Regardless, they are proud of a child who studies and works hard.*

Parents cherish a child who is attending a university. It brings them a sense of pride and accomplishment. As for the comment about differences of opinions on selecting a major, I have heard similar observations from several students. Nowadays, a difference of opinions between parents and college age students is common in China.

> *The accurate definition of education begins to have a slight difference from what was in people's mind. In my opinion, education is the bridge between teachers and students, the mediator between the individual and society, the transmission of more knowledge to society, being a wholly developed person in society.*

These are profound words. I believe this person expresses the opinions of many young Chinese—a good education affects an individual and benefits society.

The teacher-student relationship is a unique facet of Chinese education—it is a form of extended family. In my particular situation, it is a type of father-son/daughter relationship. I particularly value students' sharing their inner thoughts. My students know I am an American and a Christian, and I hope they see me as easygoing, fun loving, considerate, and nonthreatening. More than that, I hope we develop long-lasting relationships.

AMERICA

Quite frequently, I hear my students comment about America's being a powerful nation with great scientific and technological achievements. It is a Christian nation and highly developed. Americans are people with a lot of freedom of choice and a lust for life. They are over six feet tall with blonde hair and blue eyes. When they are eighteen years old, they can leave their parents and live on their own. American college students have much more freedom on campus than Chinese students. The list goes on.

However, I do not fit the stereotypical mold of the tall American with blonde hair and blue eyes. I am a Mexican-American, short, with a medium build and gray hair. One day while I was inside an office building, waiting to catch an elevator to a dentist office, a security guard approached me and asked me what country I came from. I told him America. He said, "You can't be American. You are too short." I remember the surprised looks on my students' faces when they saw me for the first time and I told them I was an American. Some thought I was from somewhere in the Middle East.

Student Comments

> Well, I do not know Americans very well, but in my mind America is crazy with freedom and liberty. Americans are people easy to communicate with and have outgoing characteristics. America is a land full of legends. You are a people who have courage, confidence, and an adventurous spirit.

American liberty and freedom are of interest during discussions about the United States. Some students envy such attributes of a country and wish they had more of them. There is also an interest in the "American Spirit." I had one student in a class who made a hobby of studying American history.

> *Americans can do what they want to do. Maybe I was greatly affected by the movies produced by the U.S. I look forward to the American way of life. As for me, the Americans are unconditional and open-minded. Americans are rich. In the movies, I see you all drive cars, eat fast food, and drink beer. You are all very busy for life. You like moving from one place to another. I think your life is much unrestrained.*

The power of the American media—Americans drive cars, eat fast food, and drink beer. In some respects, I must say these stereotypes hold true, of course. I might add that for some reason many Chinese see all Americans as being wealthy, and that to become wealthy is the goal of many students. They want a rich and prosperous future.

> *In my opinion, Americans are very open and independent. American students have to do part-time jobs to earn money for the summer holiday. In school, they learn about many different subjects we never heard of before. I think it is very interesting. Compared with them, I think our study life is a little boring. American parents are also very open; they give their children free space to grow. Besides, I think Americans are very good at enjoying life.*

Actually, there is a bit of envy from Chinese students when it comes to American students' lifestyles. That American parents give their children space to grow is a concept with which all my students agree. Although they are in university, parental influence still has a firm grip on their lives.

> *I think Americans make a good impression on me. Their life is more independent and free. They have a good sense of time. They will schedule their own affairs in advance, which gives them a better life. I think if there was a chance, I would like to enjoy their life.*

Interesting how this student focuses on Americans scheduling their affairs in advance. In my observations, especially as a teacher, the Chinese frequently schedule meetings at the last minute or at an inconvenient time. Perhaps this student has reached the point of intolerance. New and veteran foreign teachers share mixed feelings about this kind of time management. I can tolerate it at times but only with a "grin and bear it" approach.

Americans are fashionable and evil. From the computer I can see stories about the percentage of high crime in America.

Not all students have positive views. When one student called George W. Bush a war criminal, I was startled until I found out he had read the text on the Internet in English, translated from an Iraqi newspaper. My teaching experience in China has prepared me for such negative comments about America. I usually let the students share their opinions, whether I agree with them or not.

America is a democratic country. Americans enjoy more political rights and are therefore more concerned about political rights and political issues. I am not sure what China should do in order to advance on the route of democracy and the freedom of the media, but it definitely needs to move forward. The press in the U.S. enjoys more freedom and is less controlled by the government. That is my view about the U.S. society.

It took a lot of courage for this student to share these comments, especially in the presence of classmates. It is possible this lonely student received criticism from classmates outside of class. I am not in China for political reasons, but I find these sentiments powerful and perhaps shared by other Chinese students.

Chinese university students' fascination with America is amazing. Let me conclude this section with a story. I scheduled two hours a week for Office Hours, a time when students can come into my office, practice their English, ask questions, and speak their minds. A male student frequently used this opportunity to ask for peculiar information, such as the number of freshwater bodies in America, the different kinds of trees, the names of all the historical cities and landmarks, the percentage of ethnic populations in America, and so on. I suppose he felt that, as an American, I would have all the answers. I would evade the questions by asking for some time to think about the answer and present it the following week. Finally, after several weeks of this unceasing drill, I gave the student a gift. Chinese do not normally open gifts the moment they are given. They see giving and receiving a gift as a private matter. I encouraged the student to open my gift. It was an almanac. He gleamed with pleasure. I told him it contained everything he wanted to know about America.

CONCLUSION

My cross-cultural experience reminds me of a story I heard during a Sunday morning service I attended during a furlough in the United States. A young seminary graduate student and a well-known elderly pastor sat next to each other during a Sunday service. As the pastor of the church approached the pulpit to give the morning sermon, the elderly pastor, waiting in anticipation, had his Bible, notepad, and pencil at the ready. Puzzled, the seminary student looked at him and said, "You have studied the Bible for many years, know more about it than the pastor of this church, and probably have read the same passages many times. Why are you still taking notes?" Slowly the elderly pastor turned to the student and said, "One should never stop learning." I am mindful of these words while entering a classroom with lessons prepared and ready to teach. There sit my teachers, whose lessons about Chinese culture require no formal preparation, but rather, are lived. I am indebted to these young minds for giving me this ongoing cultural education which has captivated my heart.

10

Hospitality

by Emily Ciccotti

I WAS ENJOYING A midyear conference in warm, sunny Thailand while my home in south-central China was experiencing the worst snow-storm in fifty years, according to media accounts. Trains had stopped running. Buses were stranded by the side of the road. Thousands of people in the industrial cities of Guangzhou and Shenzhen were camped out at the stations hoping for tickets. All wanted to go home for the single most important holiday of the year: Spring Festival.

Spring Festival is the celebration of the lunar New Year. Families pull out all the stops to prepare a fantastic feast of foods rich in flavor and meaning. It is a time for visiting relatives, giving children gifts of money in red envelopes, and setting off fireworks. My former student Alicia had been inviting me to visit her home for the last year and a half, and I finally had time to make the trek out to her village home in Jiangxi Province. But with the severe weather reports I was receiving in Thailand, I wondered how I would get there. In the Chiang Mai airport waiting to depart, I wrote Alicia an email asking if it was still okay for me to come, clicked "send," boarded the plane, and began an unforgettable journey.

I arrived in Shenzhen in southern China a little later than scheduled and immediately contacted Liu, who had arranged some of the details for my stop in Shenzhen. Liu lived in my Chinese home of Changsha, a friend of a friend. When I had shared with my friend in Changsha that I didn't know a good place to stay in Shenzhen, she thought of Liu, who was visiting friends there. He agreed to help me out. He actually didn't anticipate being in Shenzhen when I returned, but he was going to ask his friends to work things out and take care of me.

In China, as the proverb goes, plans cannot keep up with change. Because of the terrible ice storm Liu's friends couldn't go home for the festival, and Liu decided to keep them company. When I texted him upon my arrival in the airport, he contacted his friend's business acquaintance who was waiting at the airport to meet me and help me to the hotel that they had reserved for me. Following an exchange of chinglish text messages, Mr. Po found me and hailed a taxi to take me to the hotel. We traveled mostly in silence to the hotel, a five-minute ride from the airport. I was tired and felt quite indebted that someone who didn't even know me had taken the time to help me at this late hour. Once at the hotel he checked me in, saw that I had all that I needed, and left. I was not quite sure what would happen next, but I understood that I should go to bed and find out the next step in the morning.

The characters in this account form a tangled web that may prove difficult to keep straight. But in a sense, that quality reflects the social networking in Chinese culture. One needs something and has a friend who can't help. But the friend has a friend who has a friend who knows someone who can help. This may help to explain why I trusted Mr. Po to find me at the airport and take me to a darkly lit hotel at midnight. Because, in fact, my trust in Mr. Po's goodwill was based on my trust in my friend back in Changsha, from whom this web of "friends" began.

The next day Liu told me Mr. Po would again escort me to the train station and help me buy a ticket. When we got to the train station, he left me sitting by a pillar and joined the droves of migrant workers and other Shenzhen residents waiting in anxious hope of obtaining a train ticket home for what was left of the holiday. A couple hours later Mr. Po returned with a prized ticket. It was not exactly the ticket I had been hoping for. I had wanted to leave Shenzhen that day but this ticket was for the following afternoon, and I had hoped for a seat or a bed but this was a standing ticket. I took a deep breath as I thought about the nine-hour trip that I would spend standing and did my best to express to Mr. Po how grateful I was to even *have* a ticket.

The next day Liu accompanied me back to the train station, helping me carry my heavy luggage. We wove our way through the station to the waiting area for my train. At this point in my encounter with Liu, my reservoir of small talk was beginning to dry up and my thoughts wandered to the next leg of my journey. *I've never had a standing ticket for such a long trip. I'm traveling alone. People are going to be staring at me because*

I'm a tall Westerner. They're going to think I'm crazy to be traveling by myself and with so much luggage. I'm dreading this part of the trip . . . Why am I doing this? Of course, I'm excited to see Alicia. But these next hours are not going to be fun. I tried not to show Liu how nervous I was because I didn't want him to worry or to think that I was ungrateful for the tremendous amount of help he and his friends had given me over the last thirty-six hours.

When the time came for me to board, Liu shouldered some of my luggage and hustled me into line, hoping to find me a comfortable spot to stand in my car. I followed, biting my lip in an effort to hold back tears. Once in the car, Liu spotted a few college-aged girls and told them my situation. I was standing behind him feeling self-conscious as the many pairs of curious black eyes watched the situation. The girls kindly agreed to let me squeeze onto the edge of their seat. After stowing my luggage on the rack above the seats, Liu said a quick goodbye and was off.

As soon as he was gone, the tears began to flow. One of the girls handed me a tissue but otherwise they looked quite unsure of what to make of the situation. My emotions subsided after my eyes had leaked out the stress of the unknown and of all the insecurities I had been feeling about cultural encounters I did not understand.

Minutes ticked by and the girls around me were cordial but mostly did their own thing, perhaps too shy to communicate with this foreigner. The passengers across the way, however, were a little more curious. I could understand snippets of their queries. One man said, "Where do you think she's from?"

"Maybe America or Russia," another answered.

I ventured to start a conversation with the only girl among them. "*Ni hao*" (Hello), I awkwardly began.

"She can speak Chinese!" the men murmured.

"I can speak a little," I replied.

"Where are you from?" one of them asked.

"I'm from America, but I'm studying Chinese in Changsha," I explained.

"Oh, you speak very standard Mandarin," the man continued. This is a common compliment given to foreigners.

"Do you live in Shenzhen?" I asked the girl.

"Yes, I work there," came her cautious reply. "This is my brother."

"*Ni hao.*" I greeted the young man who was wearing a sharp navy blue suit complemented by a shiny maroon tie.

He smiled a sheepish grin and replied in Mandarin, "I can't speak English. I've never had the opportunity to study English."

"It doesn't matter. We can use Chinese," I said.

"You are the first foreigner I've met."

"Where are you from?" I asked.

"I work in a factory in Shenzhen. I live with my older sister."

"Where are you two going now?" I continued small talk.

"We're going home to celebrate Spring Festival with our family."

"Where is your home?" I continued asking the basic questions I had been learning in my Chinese classes that semester.

"Our home is outside of Nanchang in Jiangxi Province."

"Oh, I used to live there! I taught English at a university."

"Really?! Which university?"

"Jiangxi Blue Sky University."

"I know which one you are talking about. I would also love to study English."

"Really? I can teach you right now." I could tell by his sheepish smile he was still nervous, but when I offered to teach him English, his eyes lit up. So I pulled out my little red travel notebook and started with the introductory phrase:

"Hello. How are you?" I placed my finger under each word, saying it slowly as he looked at the letters. I repeated the process then said, "Now you try it."

"Hallo." He hesitantly repeated the word.

"Hello," I repeated, this time emphasizing the short /e/ sound. After three or four repetitions he was starting to get the hang of it. We moved on to "How are you?"

"Sheesh, English is hard!" he exclaimed in Chinese.

I tried to encourage him in my broken Chinese. I then proceeded to teach him, "My name is . . ." Interspersed with our little English lesson was friendly banter and a continued effort to communicate about our lives using a mixture of our two languages and the help of the girl in the next booth.

When seven o'clock rolled around, my new friend brought out rolls and milk. He offered me some, which I tried to refuse. But he insisted on sharing his dinner with me. I felt so welcomed and accepted by this young friend that my earlier feelings of fear and loneliness had evaporated. Over the last few hours of our journey, we shared only intermittent snippets of conversation, but now there was the friendly air of community. At around eleven p.m. my new friend nudged me and said, "You can sit in my seat for a little while."

"It's okay. I don't need to. It's your seat." I tried to refuse. But he stood up insisting that he was tired of sitting. I was so exhausted and my bum so sore from sitting on the edge of a seat that I finally accepted his offer and dozed for an hour while he stood. As we rolled into Ji'an station, I asked my friend, *"Ni keyi bang wo ma?"* Can you help me? I motioned to my bag above the seat. Without hesitation, he helped me to get my luggage off the overhead rack.

Stepping through the exit gate, I soon spotted the short thin form of Alicia, a no-nonsense girl who loves life and the outdoors, characteristically outfitted in jeans and a padded windbreaker, hair pulled back in a pony tail. She greeted me with a hug and hustled me down the ramp to the little motel built into the station. We walked over the threshold past a sleeping attendant and up to the desk by the stairway. The second attendant's hazy and slightly irritated facial expression matched the hour, and after Alicia exchanged a few words with him, we trooped up the creaky wooden stairs and down a hall to the room we would occupy for the next few hours.

We set down the luggage, brushed our teeth, and tried to get ready for bed. We stripped down to our long underwear bottoms, but it was so cold that we both slept in our jackets, me with my hood up in an effort to conserve every bit of body heat from the cold seeping in from the window frames and loosely constructed walls. In the middle of the night Alicia whispered, "Emily, can I get in the bed and sleep with you? I'm too cold."

Only half awake I rubbed my eyes and replied, "Of course." We huddled together in the narrow twin bed, moments later drifting back to sleep.

The next morning I took the last hot shower I would enjoy for the next four days and then began to pack up my things.

Alicia was visibly uncomfortable. "Emily, I'm a little worried that you will not like my home."

"Why wouldn't I like your home?" I asked.

"My family doesn't have much money. We live in a village." She continued, trying to explain her concerns while honoring her family.

"That's okay. I have been to a village before and I love village life." I tried to ease her fears.

"But it's not like the city," she pressed.

"Hmm, do you mean like the bathroom isn't the same?"

"Yes! It's not like a bathroom in the city. We don't have a shower like the one in the hotel."

"That's okay. I have been to places that don't have city bathrooms, and I don't have to take a shower every day."

"Really? You don't mind not taking a shower?"

"I really don't mind. One time I was on a wilderness trip and I didn't take a shower for three weeks."

"Okay."

"Alicia, please let me experience your everyday life in the village. One time I visited my Chinese brother's village, and he didn't let me experience everything because I was a foreigner and he wanted me to be more comfortable. But I really want to experience everything. I'm sure I will like it very much."

"Are you sure?"

"Yes," I replied with firm sincerity.

"Okay, I will let you experience my life. But there will be some things that I think my mother will not want you to do. But I will try," she decided.

"Thank you! I am very excited!"

"Okay, I think we need to hurry. My family is waiting for us." After two buses and a half-mile walk, we were dropped off at an open-air market on the outskirts of Wujiang. We wandered among the roped-off areas to where Alicia's father sat surrounded by several large basins of live fish. He was a thin wiry man sporting a navy blue stocking cap to ward off the winter chill. He greeted us with a warm toothy smile and shining eyes, crow's feet etched into his leathery skin, revealing the life of a hard-working farmer with a warm heart. After a brief introduction a friend of a relative took us by scooter half a mile on a paved road and turned left down a dirt road.

Upon our arrival Alicia's mom and brother lit a string of firecrackers. I felt so honored! Alicia told me it was a tradition to set off firecrackers whenever a guest or family member comes to visit during the festival. We then sat down to a meal of around fifteen dishes, including several kinds of meat and fish. It's Chinese custom to have lots of meat and fish during the festival, as they symbolize wealth and well-being. The meal had abundance and variety, the kind of which I had not seen in a long time. Alicia did me the "favor" of telling me what was in each dish. I've since decided that it's sometimes easier to eat strange food if I don't know what it is. One of the dishes was spicy dog meat. It was a first for me but God graciously helped me to be culturally appropriate and taste what was given me, and I must say the flavor was good.

When Alicia's dad came home, we sat down for a few minutes to chat and warm our hands by the fire in their living room. They had recently built a new two-story house in which they have their bedrooms and a main room with a table and a television, though Alicia's mom still cooked in the old house and the family still ate in the kitchen and hung out in the living room. There was a small fire in the center of the room with small wooden chairs scattered around and whole fish and sides of meat smoking above. I felt as if I were in a homestead in America during the 1800s. As we warmed our hands, Alicia's mom passed around oranges wrapped in cellophane for us all to enjoy. Then Alicia's dad said, "Zhao Yu Xiang (Alicia's Chinese name) has told me you are like sisters."

"Yes," I replied with a big smile.

"If you are sisters, then can I be your Chinese dad?" he continued. I was caught off guard but his question was so sweet. Alicia clarified saying,

"He wants to know if when you are in the China he can be your father."

"Okay!" I readily agreed. I didn't know what it meant, but I thought it would be neat to have a Chinese father.

"*Ni keyi jiao wo 'Gan Baba'*" (You can call me "adoptive dad"), he explained. There was even a specific word for surrogate parents! I had "adopted" a few Chinese brothers and sisters myself. But this was the first time someone had adopted me as his daughter in my new country.

No sooner had lunch begun to settle than we were out the door on scooters to a relative's house. I was introduced to several family members, and then we sat down to an even larger feast. This house was made of wood with a high ceiling and dirt floor. There were chickens pecking around under the table. In one corner they had built a fire on the floor with chairs all around, similar to Alicia's home. After the meal the young cousins, boys of about four or five years, lit sparklers inside the house and had fun clowning for the camera as I took video footage of them. They got such a kick out of seeing themselves.

We returned to Alicia's home later that afternoon, had a light dinner, and then hung out around the fire. I trained my ears to catch some meaning of the family's light banter. They would make comments and then one of them would exclaim, *"Shuo putonghua!"* (Speak Mandarin!) so that I could understand. Alicia's mom said, "Alicia, give your teacher oranges."

Alicia then asked me, "Do you want an orange?"

"Sure!" I replied as she passed me a couple of small tangerine-like oranges wrapped in cellophane. *"Zhe xie juzi feichang hao chi!"* (These oranges are so good!) I said to Gan Mama. Gan Mama had only been able to attend school for one year so she spoke only a little Mandarin, severely limiting our ability to communicate verbally.

Alicia's brother Lili was sixteen and normally attended boarding school in Jishui, one of the small towns nearby. He said to his sister with a proudly confident air as if he were the older, more experienced one, "Your pronunciation is not good!"

Alicia was visibly bothered so I asked, "What did he say?"

"He said my pronunciation is not good," Alicia translated.

"Huh, I'm your English teacher and I think your pronunciation is good."

She turned to Lili with a victorious grin. "She said my pronunciation is very good!" Lili was momentarily silenced.

"My Chinese is not good," I said. So Gan Baba came around and sat beside me with his fantastic smile.

"Okay, I'm going to teach you Chinese." Gan Baba had gone to school through sixth grade. He took the fire poker and slowly wrote "公园" in the ashes beside the fire. As he made each stroke he spoke the pinyin slowly, *"Gong yuan."*

"Oh, I see! Thank you for teaching me Chinese!" My Gan Baba was really making the effort to connect with me, even though my Chinese of one semester was very limited and he spoke no English.

That night we brushed our teeth out on the edge of the packed dirt courtyard where there was a rugged cement sink and a spigot, their only fresh water source. We washed our faces and feet in a basin Gan Mama had warmed for us. Alicia gave me a flashlight so that I could find my way to the "outhouse." The toilet was a big pit about four feet by four feet hidden from the courtyard by a wall.

The next morning Gan Mama reheated dishes from the day before, steaming them over a wok. During the winter she put leftovers into a cupboard—no need for a refrigerator. Breakfast was huge. In addition to the leftovers, Gan Mama had a made a huge bowl of rice porridge, boiled eggs that had been freshly laid by her hens, and deep-fried chewy pumpkin cakes. There was no way I would go hungry here! "The pumpkin cakes are very good," I told Gan Mama.

She replied with a big smile, "Eat a little more!"

As Alicia and I sat down to eat, Gan Baba came in and started teaching me words from their dialect. He pointed to the boiled eggs and said, "Egg is *'bobo.'*"

"*Bobo*," I repeated.

"Yes, in our dialect, egg is *'bobo*,'" he reiterated. Then he pointed outside to where the chickens were and continued the lesson, "Chicken is *'jidei.'*"

"*Jidei*," I imitated.

"And, duck is *'yadei'*".

"Oh, I see, *yadei*." After breakfast Alicia, knowing that I loved hiking, had planned a trip to a small mountain near her relative's village. So Lili took us on the family scooter down a dirt road to Gan Mama's niece's house. We hung out with the women and children and enjoyed a snack of rice cakes and a special kind of tea made of ground peanuts, sesame seeds, and green tea leaves. The open hospitality was warm and welcoming. I also enjoyed a glimpse of Lili's affection for his little cousin as he swung him up into his arms.

We continued down another dirt road that led to the base of the mountain. It was a fun hike as we could enjoy the fresh air and I got to observe more of the playful banter between Alicia and Lili.

When we arrived back home, Gan Baba had his fishing pants on and was preparing to catch fish for the relatives from his rice field. The field is normally full of water from a pond situated a few feet above the field. When Gan Baba wants to catch fish, he opens a little gate and releases water from that field into another one that is a foot or two below the fish farm. He then just reaches down in between the rice stalks and picks up the fish.

That night the family gathered again around the fire with plenty of oranges and pumpkin seeds to go around. Alicia, Lili, and Gan Baba decided to play cards. Since I was unfamiliar with the game, I opted to watch the first few rounds. As I watched, I picked up a few more words of their dialect. Lili threw down a card and said, "*Shee.*" He was saying the number ten in their dialect, a slightly different pronunciation than in Mandarin—"*shi,*" which sounds like "sure" in English. The evening wore on and we finally decided it was time for bed.

The next day Alicia was busy, so I hung out with Gan Mama and Lili. Gan Mama told Lili he needed to wash his clothes, a task he was less than excited about. I was curious to see how they washed clothes with the basin and washboard, so I asked him to teach me. This motivated him a little. After letting me try for about five minutes, he insisted on finishing the task, embarrassed that a guest was doing his laundry for him.

After Lili finished his laundry, he took me to explore the little hills in the area. We poked around for a while and then decided to head home through the orange orchard. The family owns about two-thirds of a huge orchard in front of their house, which, with the fish farming, provides a livelihood. At home we had a simple but delicious lunch of noodle soup. Then Lili and I pulled out our textbooks, he his English homework and I my Chinese language book, and we studied together. As a snack I brought out packets of hot chocolate and Tim Tams that I'd brought from Thailand to share with the family. I taught them the "Tim Tam Slam," where you suck hot chocolate through the cookie until it's mushy and then quickly gobble it up before it breaks off into the mug, all without using your hands. Gan Mama was the only successful Tim Tam Slammer among us!

Later in the afternoon, one of Alicia's high school friends Alice came over to spend the night. Gan Mama let me set off the firecrackers to welcome her! While Gan Mama was preparing dinner, Alicia, Alice, and I drank hot water and sat around the fire chatting about the differences in pronunciation between British and American English. When Gan Baba finished his work with the fish, he went into his room and came back with a red envelope for me. I pulled out two small bills. One was a red one-yuan note with a girl riding a tractor and a shepherd with a flock of sheep on the back. The other was a green, worn and torn two-yuan note that had been taped together. There was a worker in overalls leaning over a piece of machinery on the front and something resembling an oil field on the back. They were both dated 1960. Gan Baba explained that they were very old, from the time of the revolution. This Spring Festival gift was a very special keepsake from my Gan Baba to his adopted daughter.

Receiving this gift from my Gan Baba on top of all the wonderful hospitality and honor the family had shown me left me racking my brain for some other gift I could give them to show my love for them. I had given Gan Mama a set of incense and scented soap, but it just didn't seem like enough. The only thing I had with me was my well-used compact Chinese/English-English/Chinese Dictionary. I felt bad that it was not new and polished, but I knew it was better than Lili's current one, so I gave it to him. Lili and Gan Mama seemed touched.

The next morning Alicia and I packed up our bags and headed to town to catch the bus to to Ji'an and ultimately to Nanchang, where she would return to her university and I would visit other old friends.

Two years have passed since I visited Wujiang. Gan Baba called me a few days ago and invited me to return to my adopted Chinese home for the New Year. I'm hoping to make it so that I can introduce my husband to my Chinese family.

11

The Language of Love

WHY MANDARIN ISN'T THE ONLY LANGUAGE I SHOULD HAVE STUDIED BEFORE MOVING TO CHINA

by Lindsey Paulick

LOVE IS INTERNATIONAL—WITH AS many diverse cultural manifestations as there are languages in the world. This ubiquitous reality can range from our Western romantic expectations of flowers and love songs to Shakespearean tragedies and their counterparts in cultures around the world, including China. As I've spent the last year teaching at a Chinese university and observing relationships all along the spectrum of romantic, parental, and platonic love, I've discovered that love in China has done more than surprise me; it has opened my closed American heart to ways of expressing love in ways I never would have imagined.

The first thing that assaulted my senses after arriving in Baoding was not the sights or the smells, for which people had prepared me. My new home, Baoding—a small bustling city with a population of just over one million people barely eighty kilometers southwest of Beijing—boasts a history that goes back more than a thousand years. Though it stands in stark contrast to the modern metropolis of Beijing today, in its heyday during the Yuan Dynasty it served as the south entrance to the capital city. Government officials resided here in luxurious homes and ate delectable dishes created for their enjoyment and known only to Baoding. I expected the aromas of the centuries to fill my nose and the ancient city walls to fill my imagination with pagodas dotting the tree-filled horizon and peasants wandering the streets in triangular bowl hats and bare feet.

To my dismay, I awoke the morning after my late-night arrival to find a dirty little city full of rubble—apparently as part of Baoding's ten-year beautification plan most of the older building are being razed—and noise. Lots of noise. Firecrackers started at six a.m. and were my alarm clock for the next three months until I learned to sleep through them. As I began my first car-less year since I was in high school and took off on the little—and I mean little—yellow bike generously provided by the university, I felt my heart skip and stop at every bike-bell chime and honk of the horn. Horn-honking was not a language I had studied before coming to China. Apparently though, it is much more a language of love than any sort of honking I have ever heard in America. In fact, the incessant horn honking is actually a sign of careful and courteous driving—the drivers are just letting you know they're behind you so you don't get hit.

At first, I couldn't keep myself from laughing at the cat-like reflexes of the taxi drivers letting out torrents of fist-pumps on the steering wheel every time a pair of eyes wandered into the general direction of the path of their vehicle. Yet as I learned to maneuver my way through dense crowds of teal-colored taxis, mule-pulled carts, and rusty bikes, it dawned on me that their horn-honking habit directly reflected their concern for the people of their city. See, in China, the cool thing about riding a bike is *you can do whatever you want.* No one is going to think you're crazy for darting out into the middle of the intersection between cars and trucks to wait on the narrow yellow line separating you from on-coming traffic. This is how you cross the street. No one will look at you funny for riding on the "wrong side of the road," whatever that means. Outside of more modern cities like Shanghai and Beijing, traffic laws are more suggestions than absolutes. Bike helmets and seat belts haven't quite caught on. So, here's the not-so-cool part. Dangerous and deadly accidents involving automobiles, buses, motor-scooters, and especially bicycles, are everyday occurrences. China holds the unenviable distinction as the country with the most fatal accidents annually. More than 650 people are killed and 45,000 injured *every day,* according to the World Health Organization (WHO). Though they may not know these statistics, taxi drivers are certainly witnessing these tragic realities on a weekly basis, so they have done well to develop this warning system/love language.

As I ride on the right side of the narrow two-lane road lined with vendors and pedestrians, I listen for the bumps of the horns that say, "I'm coming up on your left." When people stop in the middle of the road and divert the flow of traffic so that I'm forced to ride on the wrong side of the road into oncoming taxis, I don't assume anymore that the taxi-drivers aimed right at me and blaring their horns are annoyed at my careless biking. Instead, I know they are concerned for my safety and want to make sure I am getting out of the way before they whiz by. This honking is different from the aggressive, angry sounds that come from the traffic jams in Los Angeles, where I spent my formative driving years, so it has taken some reconditioning to keep my reaction to a minimum. This is not to say that no one ever honks their horns out of pure frustration in China. But I'm learning to question my reactions and withhold judgment while looking for a reason to explain the phenomenon.

I soon had another opportunity to put this lesson into practice as the excitement of being in a new country began to wear off and the underlying collision of cultures began to surface. As a single independent American woman, I have traveled all over the world, often alone, including several solo trips to Asia. So, though I was informed in advance that Chinese hospitality would help me with "anything I needed," I was not prepared for how much their gracious acts of care and concern would irritate me. I should be thankful and happy that my hosts always insist on escorting me to my door, even if it is a mere five-minute walk from the classroom to my apartment. I should be touched that after catching my first Chinese cold, my new friends insisted on coming over to make noodles, force-feed me tar bottled as cough syrup, and put me back to bed hours before I was ready, sweating, not from a fever but from all the extra blankets they piled on top of me. Instead, I had to suppress child-like urges to scream, "I'm a big girl! I can do this myself!" I learned to keep my colds to myself from then on, trying to hold sneezes in until after class. But I also learned how deeply important physical care is in expressing affection for one's friends and family in China.

When I have given lectures to my students on the Five Love Languages and asked them to identify a time when they felt most loved, I would hear answers like "My mom text messages me every day to remind me to wear a coat" or "I had my tonsils out and my parents brought me homemade soup to school for a month, though soup was readily available at the school cafeteria." Likewise, when the weather turned cold,

I received several messages from my friends and students reminding me to wear a suitable jacket and scarf, and they have scolded me more than once for wearing cropped pants outside when it was an icy sixty-six degrees. When I have walked through a courtyard in the middle of campus with a group of students, without fail they would grab my arm and exclaim, "Take care!" as they pointed to the small step leading up to the gate. Most of the students whom I've asked say they never say "I love you" to people in their family. But they have no doubt that they are loved because of the constant care-taking and service offered by their parents.

After repenting of my prideful irritation, I felt inadequate to take care of my friends the way they care for me, limited as I am in the language and in knowledge of the culture. When I expressed this, they would always reply to the effect of "Don't worry about it! You can take care of me when I am in your country, but while you are here, it's my duty to take care of you." Now I can graciously accept their service and pray that one day I will have the opportunity to show at least some of them the kindness they have shown me. Until then, I can say thank you, though not too often.

One of the hardest habits to break, as my parents did a really thorough job of teaching their children proper American manners, has been that of repeating "Thanks" and "Thank you" whenever someone goes out of his or her way for me. Because of the common love language of service, I constantly have friends who volunteer to do such things as help me fix my computer, take me to get my hair cut, or buy my train tickets. But I have been scolded more than once by these friends to "Stop saying thank you!" It is offensive to them because it makes our relationship sound more formal than it is. They help me because as my friend, it is their duty and, because I am a foreign guest, it is their honor. Love is never detached from responsibility.

Doing something for a friend because you feel you are supposed to doesn't necessarily diminish the affection behind the action. In America, there seems to be this expectation that you should do something for someone you love only when the feeling of love overflows into heartfelt action. Otherwise it is merely obligation, not love. That does not seem to be the case in China. Girlfriends help their boyfriends' friends with their English homework to the point of actually completing it for them. (It is comical to bust students for cheating and find out one girlfriend wrote five incredibly similar essays.) This is the duty of girlfriends, and even if the girls don't like it, they comply out of love for their boyfriends. It's not just females, though. A young Christian brother I know is currently wracked with guilt and fear for helping his friend cheat on an exam by throwing answers on little crumpled pieces of paper across the room. He felt he had no choice but to fulfill his responsibility to his friend, who supposedly would have failed without his help. When I was in Shanghai visiting a Chinese friend, I was stupid enough to go through a crowded square with a backpack on my back and pretty quickly got my wallet stolen. While I scolded myself for making such a beginner's mistake, my dear friend was apologizing to me for not watching out for me and spent the next two hours after I left looking through trash cans in case the thief had discarded my wallet. After touching acts like these, it is nearly impossible for me to keep my "one expression of thanks per favor" rule—more thanks just pour out! I never would have thought I'd have to unlearn my most ingrained manners in order to care for my budding friendships in these cross-cultural situations.

One of my greatest shocks about this whole love business in China came after developing close relationships with a few married women. I was delighted to find it is the same even on the other side of the world—women love talking about their relationships, especially their relationships with men. Curious about the whole dating to marriage journey of the modern Chinese woman, I began asking some of my favorite questions: How did you meet your husband? What was the dating part like? and What made you want to marry him? To this last question I got an answer so shocking to my Hollywood-saturated American ears, I think I momentarily stopped breathing.

The initial stage of courtship seemed similar to dating in America. Most of these women met their husbands through friends or on an Internet dating site. Some even met in a surprising way. You can walk through a park on an average Sunday afternoon and see rows of laminated paper strung between trees, on which are profiles of single men and women, including all sorts of personal information such as salary, weight, and cell-phone numbers. Most often, it is a concerned mother or grandmother who peruses the profiles to find a good candidate for her child's future spouse and will then set about to arrange the meeting. However the initial meeting happens, the dating process is pretty similar to what I have witnessed in the States. Prospective mates talk a lot on the phone, go out to dinner, and spend time with each others' friends and family.

But, the question "What made you want to marry him?" got this same response not just once, but multiple times as I tested out the veracity of what I was hearing from all my married friends and acquaintances. "He's not good-looking," said my beautiful friend from the south of China. Celia, a local northern Chinese woman, giggled and said, "Well, look at him. He's not very handsome." I repeated the question, rephrased it, restated their answers, trying to come to some understanding of this strange phenomenon. They married their husbands *because* they were ugly. I must be missing something! So I took this question in the form of a game to my own population of willing survey participants—my one hundred female freshmen English majors. All but one brave soul responded the same way: they wanted to marry someone ugly. I interrupted the game to press the issue. Surely you don't really *want* to marry someone who is ugly. The one and only girl brave enough to admit she would prefer a handsome husband finally shed some light on the issue. Women want an ugly husband because a handsome, virtuous man does not exist. It is a well-accepted fact that a man cannot be both handsome and have a good job and strong character. This may come from a deeply ingrained belief in limited resources: you can only have so much of a good thing. If you have to choose between a good, but ugly man and a bad, but handsome one, of course you should choose the ugly one! When I announced to the class that I was holding out for the whole package deal, a few gasped in admiration while the rest of the class looked on me with the pity reserved for a life-long spinster. I have never before felt so American.

When I traveled to Shenzhen, a wealthy, modern city just an hour from Hong Kong in the south of China, I enjoyed the hospitality of some students from Baoding. In the way of true Chinese hospitality, they put me in a nice hotel (their own home was overcrowded because of relatives visiting for Spring Festival), paid for all my meals, and did my laundry. Tong confided in me that he and his girlfriend were undergoing a lot of stress because her parents were not accepting of their relationship. His girlfriend, from a family with five children, had three brothers who disliked Tong at first sight because, you guessed it, he is too handsome. How could a guy as good-looking as Tong possibly be treating their baby sister appropriately? The importance of a third-party, combined with my being a foreign teacher and therefore the holder of (over)respected opinions, led Tong to ask me for a favor. Having been the benefactor of their hospitality all weekend, I had little choice but to help him by subtly conveying all the positive aspects of my friend's character and abilities to this skeptical group of protective men. Apparently, the attempt was moderately successful. Though her brothers are still a bit wary, they now at least talk to him when he comes for dinner. But deep is the stigma on the bearers of a curse that would be considered nothing less than a blessing by most Americans. Maybe some of my thinking on the matter needs to be rethought.

My thinking was challenged again when I was faced with my closest friend's dating relationship with a graduate student from Baoding. She is nearing thirty and feeling the pressure from her family to find a husband, though that has not seemed to bother her much until recently. Women in China have the statistical advantage in choice of spouse in a country where boy babies have historically been preferred over girls, resulting in a slight imbalance of the sexes. Even a slight imbalance in a population of 1.3 billion made a difference of almost 40 million more men in 2002.[1] But it is an entirely different story for Chinese Christian women who, by all anecdotal accounts and recent research, outnumber Christian men something like 3:1.[2] So when a guy from the local fellowship started pursuing her, she agreed to date him. I thought this was exciting news, so I asked her how it was going. What was he like? How are you feeling about it!? As I watched her hesitate and her face become uneasy to my very girly, very American questions, I changed them to: Wait, do you even *like* him? Do you at least *sometimes* enjoy hanging out with him?

She smiled and said, "I am not American like you. I cannot think about if I like him or not. I have to keep getting to know him and see if he is a good man."

I'm still not quite sure what to make of this conversation. I know some Chinese women, who are less constrained by Chinese tradition and more influenced by American movies, who are all about what they

1. "Women and Men in China: Facts and Figures 2004," National Bureau of Statistics, Government of China, August 2004: 10. 10 Feb 2010. < http://www.stats.gov .cn/english/statisticaldata/otherdata/men&women_en.pdf>.

2. Doyle, G. Wright, "Gender Imbalance in the Chinese Church: Causes, Consequences, and Possible Cures," Global China Center 19 Oct 2005. 10 Feb 2010. <http://www.globalchinacenter.org/analysis/christianity-in-china/gender-imbalance -in-the-chinese-church-causes-consequences-and-possible-cures.php>.

feel for their boyfriend. But I see a difference in my friend that is not un-common when it comes to love in China. There is a patience, a tolerance of what we deem lower expectations or compromised standards, but which in their minds is a natural process of love that is not dependent on the initial attraction so overemphasized in my generation in America. As with most of the lessons I have been learning this year in China, I assume there is some good on both sides of the "debate" and that both sides are somewhat blinded by their culture and traditions. Learning a language of love that so starkly contrasts with my own perceptions has challenged me in really beneficial ways. Yet at the same time, love is strong in both cultures, and both Chinese and Americans have a deep desire to express and receive it.

12

Communication

by Amanda Hostetler

W E THOUGHT WE CAME to China to be teachers. Furthermore, we desired to be ambassadors from our home congregation and to be those who would perceptively appreciate all the glories of the Middle Kingdom. Instead, all we can say with certainty is that we have become mimes.

When asked by loved ones back in America, "How goes the Chinese language acquisition?" a simple "We're struggling" is the understatement of a lifetime. From the youngest among us to the oldest in our troupe we are a formidable *tour de force* in charades. Alas, ours is the wonderful life of living cross-culturally without the benefit of that great, and often underappreciated, communication tool: language.

Just last week we were accosted by mosquitoes in our apartment. They had chosen the young flesh of our five-year-old daughter, who is—tragically—highly allergic to insect bites. She needed medicine for the over forty swollen red spots that made her scratch at herself furiously. Her almond eyes pleaded with me for relief.

So I, being the matriarch of this tribe, headed forthwith to the pharmacy at the local shopping mall. Armed with only my dramatic ability, by virtue of forgetting the all important *Mandarin Phrase Book*, I confidently strode into the shop of all things medicinal. I reasoned with myself that it would be easy enough to communicate my need for a cure-all for mosquito bites. Unlike some dastardly intestinal ailment, it was not something dark and difficult to explain!

Using my best imitation Mandarin, I first inquired if either of the shop clerks spoke English.

No dice.

Unflinchingly, I moved directly into charades mode. First I pointed to a reddish spot on my own person; never mind that it wasn't a mosquito bite, but in fact some scourge of my aging flesh. The first clerk did not savvy the subtleties of my communiqué.

I pressed on, this time turning to face the second clerk. This clerk was one of the few Chinese I've encountered who apparently disdained the foreigner's presence in her shop. However, this matter involved my young, so I had to persevere. I redoubled my effort and made a buzzing noise to simulate a blood-sucking parasite affixing itself to the hand of the second clerk.

She violently retracted her hand and turned her face away.

I was stymied, I will admit. Yet, the years of community theatre buoyed my hopes that perhaps a more dramatic impersonation of a mosquito would connect the dots for the two clerks who were now both attempting to ignore the ridiculous foreigner buzzing and flapping her arms like wings.

I backed up, revealed the red dot on my own hand, used my rudimentary Chinese to reference my child, then buzzed louder while lengthening my flight path and then mimicked a blood-sucking pest drinking its libation through a straw stuck to the hand of Clerk Number One. (He had foolishly left his hand in sight on the counter, whereas Clerk Number Two had buried her hands in the inaccessible regions of the shelf containing bowel elixirs.)

Finally, accepting my declining favor with the clerks, I did what all foreigners at times must do in China—I dialed a friend who could translate my desire into the local dialect, thereby producing the desired commercial exchange.

How different my life would be if I could only communicate.

Another example of my struggles with language.

The public restrooms in China vary greatly regarding the fixtures within them as well as the standard of cleanliness they exhibit. When first visiting China in 2006 as a family, our children were fascinated by the new demands of squatting over the floor-level plumbing, depositing the used tissue into the wastebasket rather than the toilet, and having to cover their noses or hold their breath to stave off the rising bile triggered by the often malodorous conditions.

Living in Asia, we've had to develop the habit of carrying tissue with us everywhere we go. Public restrooms do not stock tissue for their patrons. Parenting five children under the age of nine while living in Asia requires me to carry lots and lots of it. Often we stand for several minutes crowded within the waiting area angling for position for the next door that opens (as Chinese do not utilize an "everyone waits their turn" system, it is quite literally the pushiest who have the advantage.)

Including this background is necessary for me to appropriately illustrate the new low I reached this year regarding my language limitations.

One learns quickly the Chinese word for "bathroom." However, perhaps given my age-diminished language learning capabilities or possibly the number of offspring I parent, I experienced a delay in grasping the word for "toilet tissue."

We all experience those moments of urgency of needing a bathroom. I was experiencing one of those moments while standing among the dozens of woman waiting for a stall. I was rifling through my overstuffed bag filled with kids' toys, passports and just plain junk. Notably absent from my bag was any tissue (or my handy *Mandarin Phrase Book*). The impetus for my bathroom visit was roiling within my gut and I began to grow very nervous. My mind was racing about searching in vain for the Chinese word for "toilet tissue." This was a moment where I needed to communicate, post haste, and I had no language to utilize!

I scanned the masses waiting alongside me for anyone making eye contact. But restroom line-ups, whether in the West or in China, are not often places we naturally connect with our sisters.

The acrid air heavy with humidity and heat only exacerbated the rising tide of panic within me. I needed a stall, very quickly, and most certainly I needed to score some tissue immediately! Neither prospect looked hopeful as I began to envision needing a change of clothing if I were unable to make headway in the current crisis.

There was no way around my predicament. I needed the Mandarin word for toilet tissue, and I did not have it.

As in any situation when I am unable to use language I must resort to pantomime. But the gravity of my situation coupled with the necessary gestures that would be required to communicate "Toilet tissue, NOW, PLEASE" left me blushing with dread.

I tapped on the shoulder of a woman standing to my right. Smiling warmly, I half-heartedly drew the shape of a tissue. It was foolishness, I knew, because the drawing of a rectangle in the air can be construed in various ways. Awash in the reality of the motions I had to use next, my sense of decency and self-respect warred with the mental image of my demonstrating not only the shape of the tissue but the use of it.

The situation was desperate.

So, while trying to keep the eyes of the woman, who was growing impatient with this panic-stricken, riddle of a foreigner . . .

I did it.

I drew the shape of the rectangle and then snatched it from the air and used it to simulate the wiping motion on my very own person! The normally loud room grew silent while my heart beat furiously in my flaming ears.

The look of astonishment, then of violation, and ultimately of comprehension raced across the woman's face as she finally made the connection between my charades and their meaning.

We had communicated.

Rapidly she dispatched a package of tissues from her handbag and averted her eyes from me henceforth so that we would both be spared further humiliation.

If you had told me last year that I would sink to such depths in trying to communicate in a new culture and language, I probably would have never left my American home.

Ah, Language . . .

We think precious little of it when we can communicate with those around us. As parents, once our little darlings can efficiently communicate their thoughts and desires to us without our engaging in the twenty-questions guessing game, we constantly use language without any conscious thought.

How I've taken language for granted.

Living cross-culturally, we have also become aware of "identity" based upon our communicative skills. As a six-year veteran talk show host, theatre rat, and salesperson, I have always had the framework of communication as key to my identity.

Yet we have come to China and so far can only communicate, on our very best mime/broken dialect days, like eighteen-month-old babies.

When we ride in a taxi, the interviewer in me wants to know everything about the taxi driver—this unexplored life story needs to be heard. Or at the very least, I crave the opportunity to engage in the cerebral game of question and answer while attempting to decipher nuance for enhanced meaning. How fantastic that would be!

But no, we all have to settle for the simple repeated phrases that we've mastered regarding navigation to our desired location, garnished with the customary "What country we're from" and that scintillating fact that we parent a mind-boggling seven children!

The frustration with this limited, inadequate conversation builds.

I want to know from whence the driver has come! I'd like to hear if he has children and how old they are. And his parents—are they living nearby?

But all I can do is grunt unhappily and nod in agreement to the common phrases he gives me and helplessly say that I don't understand all the other colorful commentary he offers me.

Without the outlet of writing for a reader, perhaps I would implode? The belief, whether real or imagined, that there are those who read my writing and understand not only my basic communication of information but the deeper meanings within keeps me feeling at least half of my former self.

My husband, on the other hand, continues to be happier than I've ever known him. He seems to roll merrily along with the freedom that he doesn't have to communicate with someone he doesn't want to. He delights in the release from the old cultural pressures to make conversation and "say the right thing" to people he hadn't previously known.

For years in our marriage I have wanted my husband to show everyone his magnificent wit, his precise comedic timing, and his penchant for observation and commentary. Since he is the funniest, most interesting person I have ever known, I have wanted everyone to experience that about him. Yet he is unwilling to indiscriminately share more than the most basic communication with a greater audience beyond those he knows well. He is one person to the new acquaintance and still quite another to those he trusts.

This freedom from communication with the passerby or new acquaintance has surprised me many times in our first six months here. On countless occasions when we've crammed into a taxi to travel a short distance, out of the blue my husband will begin to belt out a song, loudly. Often the song is one he's creating extemporaneously; other times it's a favorite spiritual song, an old pop tune, or a "round" that he invites the rest of the family to join. It is so out of character for this man I've known as publically "quiet" that I'm shocked at each occurrence. It is a delightful by-product of the communication inadequacies that we experience.

Recently, as we prepared for a trip over the Spring Festival, a certain detail loomed large over our household—the need for haircuts.

I had, up to that point, scorned the frightening prospect of going to a salon and permitting someone to cut my hair without the benefit of precise communication. My beloved husband, however, would have had to start pinning up his hair had he not faced this fear some months ago.

So, we set out, separately, yet on the same day, to hair salons.

I, with great trepidation, selected the salon near the shopping center we frequent. It was a new place with dozens of chandeliers hanging from the ceiling and "artistic types" with totally mod hairstyles and funky attitudes sauntering around like brooding artists.

First up was the unbelievable head massage and hair wash. (Really, those of you Westerners in the hair maintenance trade in the West should adopt this fantastic feature.) I was taken to a row of reclining chairs set up like a furiously busy orthodontist's office, some ten stations in all. The smell of green tea and flowers wafted into my nostrils as I lay back after putting the towel around my neck. The bowl looked similar to the many I've been scoured in before, but this time, my head did not hang down uncomfortably. This was because there was a headrest in the middle of the bowl to relax the patron's head and neck during the massage and warm water wash. Undoubtedly, this was worth the price of admission. Only occasionally was I asked to lift my head into the washer's hand for a thorough cleaning and massaging of the back of my head.

Then I was taken to the chair.

I engaged in some charades accentuated by fragments of basic local dialect to communicate my desires to the stylist/brooding artist.

After a period of time, a protracted one at that, we reached an agreement. Unfortunately, I remained uncertain if the communication had been effective. I wondered if I would go home only after finding a new hat.

The process of the haircut was strange, as the stylist/brooding artist sat down behind me to clip my hair—no one stands to style. I was often nervous as the shears clipped away at my mane. I felt it important to stop the stylist/brooding artist a few times to reinforce instructions such as: on which side I part my hair and the desired length after the shears had passed through.

I emerged from the salon victorious, yet unsatisfied.

It was the first time in my life that I'd sat silently through a haircut.

I was pleased with the haircut. The stylist/brooding artist, "#9," also named Le Le, gave me his card and recommended that I return to see him in one month, or it could have been one year. I'm not really clear on some of the details.

I met my husband back at the apartment. We admired each other's new cuts, and the day went on.

Some two hours later my husband emerged from the bathroom, where he had evidently been taking stock of his new "do," and said, "He cut my hair wrong! He parted my hair on the wrong side! I think I have a "uni-cut." There's only one way to part this hair and it's on the WRONG side!"

After an intense visual inspection, I deemed that he was correct. He had been scalped on what should have been the "long" side and had been left too generous an amount of hair on the "part" side.

We chuckled, and he hastily took some scissors to the hair to remedy his predicament.

At the end of the day, I began to think about my husband's enjoying the freedom of sitting in the styling chair, not needing to force conversation and to mime his way to an understanding of the correct side to part his hair.

I, on the other hand, had avoided getting my hair shorn for fear of not being able to communicate my desires. Furthermore, I had frustrated #9, Le Le, Stylist/Brooding artist, with numerous attempts to direct his shears—and, had left unsatisfied, for I knew nothing about #9, Le Le, Stylist/Brooding artist. How old was he? How long had he been doing hair? And was I the first foreigner he'd ever had in the chair?

Communication in a new culture has produced two very different responses in my darling and me.

I am resolved to get a tutor and begin intensive language study so that my needs for medicine, bathroom paraphernalia, and impromptu interviews can be deftly handled. My husband certainly will begin tutoring as well, but perhaps with less enthusiasm as he has relished the liberty from small talk.

In this void of language and clear communication, a curious awareness is now mine—my identity as the "communicator" and his as the "quiet one"—each of us alternately frustrated and freed.

13

In Their Own Words

by Don and Karen Barnes

CHINA IS CHANGING RAPIDLY. In fact, in many ways, the current crop of university students are the last who will have much memory of "the old China" and will be able to say to their kids, "Why, when I was your age, I . . . !"

We recently asked our students to write essays on how China has changed in some specific aspect over the past ten years. We share some of those efforts here.

The context of these essays is that students are required to take a course in "politics" during each of their first two years in university. In a view shared by students around the world regarding most required courses, these students are generally not very enthusiastic about their politics course. However, the course is an opportunity for the authorities to "get their message out there," while sharing important information and perspectives.

STANDARD OF LIVING

In the past few years, a great number of changes have happened in China. We joined the WTO. We got the right to hold the Olympic Games in 2008. ShenZhou VI succeeded in flying into space. . . . Our motherland is developing rapidly. We can know that from the changes in our everyday life.

The changes in the standard of living are the most obvious. Let me take my hometown for example. When I was a little boy [circa 1996], my father sent my sister and me to school by bike every morning. At that time, it was a dirt road from my home to the school. It was so bumpy that you rode a bike on it just like you rode a horse. The road was covered by mud when it rained. On a windy day, the air around the road was full of dust. There were no buses in my hometown then. We had to go around the city by bike, tricycle, or motor tricycle. In our house we had only two electrical equipments—a small black-and-white TV set and a tape recorder. We even cooked meals by wood.

Now life is quite different. A highway has taken the place of the dirt road. You can visit our city by bus conveniently. My family has bought a 25-inch TV set, a refrigerator, a microwave, and a computer.

The good changes in our life come from our motherland's development. Rapid development depends on talents. So education is very important. China is making great effort in developing education. As people's lives become better, they are also willing to spend more money on education. So our education also has great changes. More and more people take part in the college entrance examination. And more and more people have the chance to study in university.

Year:	People who passed the [college entrance] exam:
2002	3,200,000
2003	3,350,000
2004	4,750,000

Besides, more and more children can receive compulsory education [through grade nine]. Now in some areas in China, the compulsory education is free. Recently, the government has discussed a revision draft of the compulsory education law. In the near future, compulsory education will be completely free in the whole of China.

The great changes in China spur us on. We are proud of being Chinese. We are working harder to make our motherland more flourishing. And it will be. But we should not forget that there are still many children who can't go to school and lots of people who live a hard life. We have just begun our journey. There is a long way to walk.

TRADITIONAL IDEAS

Along with the improvement in the living standard of the Chinese people, Chinese traditional ideas about routine life have been changing and becoming modern. Some values are changing.

The first change is in the concept of consumption. Before 1996, if people could just wear clothes, that was OK. They did not care too much about whether the clothes were beautiful or not. But now people are particular about clothing – fashion and high quality. As for food, people in the past only hoped to be full. But now, they are particular about taste and nutrition. Moreover, credit consumption has become the fashion in recent years.

Next is the idea of choosing a job. Before 1996, people wanted to find a secure job in state-run enterprises. But now, people are more concerned with how much they can earn and if their own values can be recognized. The notion of "seeking a position on the strength of one's abilities and merits and finding a job through competition" has gradually been accepted.

Still another concept which is changing is about bearing children. Some people had the traditional idea that the more sons, the greater happiness. Now, the policy "one couple, one child" has been appreciated by most Chinese families. And the policy now shifts its focus to a new concept: "Having fewer but healthier children."

Some traditional ideas, such as thrift, are a precious treasure for us. We should keep them. However, some unenlightened ideas are not good for our future development. So we should change.

EDUCATION

China is famous—or notorious—for its make-or-break examination system that supposedly presents a uniform hurdle across the land that all aspirants must clear if they are to go further in their careers. Perhaps the most famous, notorious, and arduous is the national examination taken by all high school students which determines whether or not they gain entrance into a "key" university—or any university for that matter.

Students study twelve to fifteen hours per day in their senior year in an all-out attempt to make it over the bar.

Many do—many more do not. An even larger number stumble and do not do as well as they—their parents, their teachers, and their friends—had wished or expected. The results can be pretty tough, which accounts in part for the high suicide rate among Chinese youth.

At the same time, we have found that the Chinese who stumble but survive the physical and mental trauma associated with this examination gauntlet are an especially resilient breed. They emerge from the trouble and turmoil pretty well beaten up and with the scars to show for it. And yet, they have acquired a "long view" of themselves and of life that should stand them in good stead in the future. The experience also leaves them open to discussion of other long-view issues about life.

Here is a first-person account about one of these youngsters, a freshman at Guangxi University, who submitted the essay in response to an assignment about a difficult time in her life.

"A Black Holiday"

In my memory, all holidays are colorful. Because we don't have to go to school, we can play happily. Nobody can take charge of us. However, the summer holiday in 2005 is black.

The month of June is very important for us students. We must take part in the College Entrance Examination. The mark even can decide our fate. The examination lasted two days. Before that, I was very confident. After all, I was the student who could enter some famous universities. Both my parents and my teachers were proud of me. I didn't have to worry about the exam.

The first day of the exam, it rained heavily, but it didn't affect my mood. I went to school happily, singing a song on my way. After arriving at school, I suddenly found that I forgot my student ID card. [NOTE: To minimize the chance of cheating, every student must have his/her government-issued photo ID card at the examination.]

"Oh, what should I do?" Fortunately, the time was enough. I rode my bike quickly. The road was so wet that I fell off. My clothes were dirty and my knee was hurt. Bad luck! Without caring about that, I dashed off.

Thank goodness! I was not late for the exam.

However, my hair and clothes were wet. My energy was given out. I felt rather uncomfortable. What's worse, my watch suddenly stopped.

I was puzzled: Is there a ghost? At that time, I had become superstitious. I was getting anxious, angry. My eyes were full of tears. Is it my fate? I don't believe. I don't want to believe. However, maybe that's true. Because my pencil was broken, it was hard to use.

I didn't know how I spent the rest of the time. It seemed that it was the hardest time in my life. Because of no watch, I couldn't control the speed, so that I could hardly finish.

The morning ended. What a sad ending! In the afternoon because of the terrible disaster, I couldn't manage to calm down. My heart beat without control. I felt more and more nervous. I couldn't work out the question. What should I do? I couldn't breathe. I felt dizzy. I wanted to die.

The examination ended. What a terrible ending. God played a joke on me! After a month, I knew my mark. I had no choice but to go to Guangxi University. This was not my ideal university. The whole summer holiday I stayed at home. Although the weather was very hot, I still felt cold. I couldn't see the sunshine. In my eyes, in my mind, there's only black. Depressed, dismay, sadness. I live such a life. Every minute I was in a bad mood.

Until now, the feeling of pain I had in that holiday is unforgettable. Sometimes, it may hurt my heart. But I'm no longer negative. I don't believe that the College Entrance Examination can decide my fate. I am the real host of my fate. Though Guangxi University is not so famous as others, I will try my best in the school. I will love it one day. I believe my future is bright, colorful, and not black.

As testimony to her changed outlook, this young writer has chosen the English name "Sunny."

14

Bundled-Up Babies

by Aminta Arrington

ZHANG, MY TUTOR, HAD a baby last month, a son. Her son was born by elective Cesarean section, just like all the other babies that Zhang and I know here in Tai'an. China's C-section rate is 50-60%, the highest in the world. It is ironic that this aspect of modernity has been embraced because most aspects of childbirth, a very political event in China, are governed meticulously by tradition. Throughout Zhang's pregnancy, she taught me about these traditions, which she called "The Chinese Way."

One of the most interesting is *Zuo Yuezi*. *Zuo Yuezi* is the first post-partum month—a month considered critical to the life of the new mother. During this month she should rarely leave her bed. Her mother-in-law should take care of her and the new baby. She should eat certain foods, such as soybean and pig feet soup, which will make her produce more milk. She should dress very warmly, for if she should catch cold during this month, her health will suffer for the remainder of her life.

Last week when another Chinese colleague suggested we go visit Zhang at her home, I was eager to see Zhang and the baby and to observe first-hand what *Zuo Yuezi* was all about. I asked my colleague about Chinese gift-giving traditions on these occasions.

"Usually some baby clothes or money," she replied. "I gave her some money. But since you are a foreigner, it would be better if you brought a gift."

I nodded, but wondered why my foreigner status had anything to do with it. The truth is I became acutely aware of my foreigner status during our entire visit.

When we arrived, Zhang was sitting on her bed, wearing so many layers of quilted pants and sweaters that she rivaled Santa Claus.

"I'm not completely observing *Zuo Yuezi* the traditional way," she told me. "Sometimes I go out (of the bedroom) and watch TV, and I've washed my hair."

"Have you gone outside?" I asked.

"No, of course not!" she said, looking at me strangely.

Her son (as yet unnamed) lay on the bed, as well-wrapped as she. Over his several layers of clothing was a white quilt several inches thick wrapped around him several times and tied snugly with two red strips. The baby was rarely held, for the layers of clothing and quilts at which he was the center made for an awkward bundle. In the Chinese mind all those clothes meant love and security. But in my mind they were layers of separation between mother and child.

Every once in awhile the baby cried, and Zhang's mother-in-law (called *Popo* in Chinese) would rush in and feed him, soothe him, or change his diaper. Popo was kind and devoted, lovingly caring for Zhang and the baby. As Popo changed or fed the baby, Zhang would look on and watch.

"I don't really know how to do anything with the baby," she said. "I guess Popo feels I am too weak to take care of the baby myself. But sometimes I feel as if it is someone else's baby."

In a sense, she was right. In China the baby belongs to the family, not to the mother. The one-child policy has only exacerbated this. Zhang would have no chance for independence and freedom in the raising of her son. Tradition would certainly prevail, for tradition (in the form of Popo) had moved in with her.

But as I sat there and observed the awkwardness she felt with her own child, now already nineteen days old, I thought to myself, "This is Zhang's only chance. This will be the only baby she ever has. How can this culture encourage distance between a mother and her own child?"

As Zhang, my other colleague, and Zhang's Popo discussed the baby in Chinese, I was engaged in an internal conversation in English. The passionate mother in me wanted to scream: "Why are you wearing so many clothes?! Just hold your baby. Wrap your arms around him. Let him feel the warmth of your body! Let him fall asleep with his head on your shoulder, Zhang, because that is one experience you just can't miss out on."

But the cross-cultural worker inside me said, "Why is your way better just because you are Western? Do you think you are somehow superior? How can you be so arrogant?"

I stifled all those voices, acutely aware of the weight of history and culture that lay between me and my friend. As a Westerner, I felt I couldn't give her advice because to do so would be to criticize thousands of years of Chinese tradition. I felt completely helpless. Zhang was as bound by these traditions as she was bound in her clothes.

I had always thought that China's traditions were its greatest treasure. I've been happy to have the chance to live far from the cosmopolitan big cities, deep in the heart of Shandong Province where the traditional ways are still strong. Most of our students come from rural villages, and our colleagues are only one generation from the countryside.

But this visit began to clear my rose-colored glasses. Culture can be a burden as well as a gift. China's thousands of years of history and civilization have meant layer upon layer of culture, mores, and traditions have collected like the silt in the Yellow River.

15

I Came to be Served

by Jesse Ciccotti

Islip on my mp3 player and head out the door, the crisp breeze at seven a.m. is better than a cup of coffee, as far as waking one up goes. I flip through songs until I find one that fits my mood as I depart, my mustard-yellow backpack slung over my shoulder.

It was a December Saturday in central inland China. Cass, a former graduate student in English Literature from my previous year teaching at Wuhan University, had invited me to give a weekend-long English lecture at one of the poorer middle-high schools in Hubei province, where he was volunteer-teaching for a year. I jumped at the opportunity, as it would be my first time getting out of the heavily urban setting of Wuhan.

At the corner I wait for my former student and friend Ken Hou, who will accompany me and act as my translator. Although I've been in China for a year and a half now, I have yet to really get anywhere with the language. Working at Wuhan University, a school that ranks among the top ten in China, I have little time for "frivolous" activities like language study. Teaching literature and oral English, as well as helping with speech competitions, Debate Club and a Shakespeare Drama Team, my free time is used for keeping in contact with friends and family and enjoying a little bit of "down time."

Ken arrives and we hop into a taxi that takes us to the bus station. Nothing remarkable occurs on the four-hour bus ride. We leave the expressway in Wuhan and barrel onto a provincial road (a two-lane highway), passing fields of winter vegetables, a cow led by a ring through the nose, gaggles of ducks on the shoulder, a water-buffalo pulling a small crude plow through red clay soil. During winter in southern China the ground rarely freezes, so farmers make the most of it growing hearty vegetables like wheat, rapeseed, and other greens for which I have yet to learn an English name.

Ironically, the name of the impoverished town we will visit (*Shengli*—pronounced Shung-lee) means Victory—I've been told that many small towns and villages changed their names to revolutionary themes, now going on sixty years ago. This particular little town shares in some of the violent history of that turbulent time, as well as in the hardships of today. On a high hill outside the town, a former Chinese general held an outpost during the war between Communist and Nationalist forces and carved a phrase into the side of the gray-streaked limestone that reads: 笑看乾坤 (*Xiao kan qiankun*—"Smile, watching over the world").

As we roll through the countryside, the limestone hills grow up all around us, created by an ancient coral reef stretching from China all the way down through Thailand and into the South Pacific. I don't know the first thing about Chinese agriculture, but I imagine this limestone bed and the resulting hills and mountains contribute to the challenges faced by farmers in this area. Many families in the villages around Shengli, as with most rural families in China, are sustained by what they grow on their small plots of land. Others choose to take up migrant work in the larger urban areas where the pay is comparatively better. Not uncommon, too, young women will take jobs in so-called hair salons and work the "night shift"—complete with pink fluorescent lights to indicate the kind of services offered.

After a bumpy four hours, we weave our way through foot traffic and scooters to an intersection in the middle of town. Cass is waiting for us with the other three volunteer teachers from Wuhan University, beaming his wide toothy smile, eyes sparkling.

"Hello, Jesse! We are so glad you could come! The students are so excited!" says Cass, in his robust voice, with a slight Chinese accent.

"I'm excited too, Cass! I hope I can offer them something that will be helpful."

We walk a half-mile to a small hotel. The room is simple but adequate—two twin beds, a desk with a TV, and a bathroom. The two twin beds are simple—a mattress cover-sheet, a pillow and case, and a duvet with cover-sheet. If we wear our long underwear, long socks, jacket, and a stocking cap, we should be quite comfortable. The heater in the room doesn't do much more than move cold air around, so we turn it off.

"The school is really kind in giving us a hotel room," says Ken. "It's probably a pretty big expense for the school."

"And it's a lot better than sleeping in the volunteer teachers' apartments," adds Cass. "We don't have much space, and I thought you would be more comfortable here."

We settle our few things into the room and walk another quarter mile to the school. Nearly all schools in China, from kindergarten to university, have a wall that surrounds the school property and at least one entrance that employs one or two guards at a time. On crude gray stone pillars, streaked with rust, swing sheet-metal gates large enough for a car to pass through. They look as though years ago they were painted gray, but are now more of a rusty brown, decorated with shreds of old announcements and advertisements that were glued to them. A vertical sign to the right should read in Chinese: *Luo Tian County Shengli Middle School*. But the frame is broken and the bottom part of the sign badly torn so that it reads only *LuoTian County . . .*

"Looks like they could use a lot more than just English lessons," I think to myself.

Once inside we cross a large courtyard, large enough for two crude concrete basketball courts, concrete slab ping pong tables—the "nets" made of unused bricks—and a large dirt area marked off for tug-of-war. After introductions with the school leaders, I'm given a brief tour of the school grounds, the leaders pointing out various buildings and Cass or Ken translating.

We scale two flights of stairs to the main education building. The windows are an old wood-frame style, with iron bars on the outside to prevent thieves and vandals from entering. Newspaper is taped over broken and missing panes to keep the draft to a minimum.

On the other side of the teaching building, we walk down a flight of stairs into a smaller dirt courtyard. On two sides of the courtyard stand low buildings, with windows complete with iron bars. Cass shows me his one-room "apartment."

"Normally, two volunteer teachers of the same sex would share a room," he says, "but because I'm working on my thesis they were really kind and gave me my own room."

I notice it has no heater. A single light bulb hangs by its own wire from the ceiling, which has been covered with a red, white, and blue tarp to keep out things like rain and small rodents. It has apparently done little to keep out mold.

The student dormitory stands at the end of the courtyard. The happy few whose parents live in Shengli are allowed to go home in the evenings, but most of the children live in the countryside, and for some the walk home through the hills could take more than two hours. Because these students are not able to make it home during the week, the school houses hundreds of students. Each room holds ten students. Four narrow, crudely made wooden bunk beds line the two sides of the room, and one bunk stands crossways at the back. The only bedding available, apart from the planks of the frame, is what students bring from home. In the winter months, Cass tells me, students will often pack two or three students in one bed to conserve body heat.

After the brief tour of campus, a few students and teachers, along with Cass, Ken, and me, pile into a silver sedan and a small van. A short drive through town leads us onto dirt roads, some of dubious quality, to visit a student's home. After twenty minutes of good jostling and bumping, we pull off down a smaller, single-car track that weaves its way between rice fields, stopping at the second farmstead.

The girl whose home it is leads the way to the concrete house. As we approach, we are greeted by the girl's mother. Her hair is pulled back in a pony-tail, and she wears a rough-woolen coat buttoned up as high as it will go and army-green canvas sneakers with gum-rubber soles, a common shoe for those with little means in China. The warmth of her smile dispels the cold afternoon breeze.

We enter the common living area and everyone is offered wooden mini-chairs and a Chinese teacup with a few tea leaves floating at the bottom. We sit in a circle and pass around a plate of dried sunflower seeds. As we eat the seeds, the discarded shells pile up on the concrete floor to be swept up later. The teacup is hot, and my knit gloves are insufficient to keep my fingers from burning, so I set it on the floor. Once I finish my seeds, I hold the cup to warm my fingers.

The room contains little. A light bulb dangles on a wire from its socket in the center of the room. Behind me two wardrobes act as catch-alls for various items—a bag of vegetables, two cardboard boxes, an umbrella, twine, a rolled-up mat. One of the doors is graced by a poster of S.H.E., a well-known female trio Chinese pop band. In the corner a television rests on a small wooden table, the most common gathering place for the family in many Chinese homes, particularly during Spring Festival, the Chinese New Year celebration.

The mother encourages her daughter to speak with me in English, and her face beams. English is often considered one of the necessary subjects for "getting ahead" in China. Most families hope that their English-speaking son or daughter will get a good job and secure a promising future. One of the great deficits I've realized during my first year and a half teaching in China is my lack of Chinese language ability. I can converse with Cass and Ken freely and with the other volunteer teachers to varying degrees, but anything else must be through translation. This adds to the distance I feel in being here. It reminds me that I'm a stranger from a far-away universe, twice removed by my white face *and* my inability to communicate with anything more than charades. But sitting in this cold concrete living room, the friendliness and understanding of my lack of Chinese somehow make up for the language barrier.

After the visit we pile back into the vehicles. The family stands in the road, waving. We visit a few more homes before returning to town for dinner at a nearby restaurant. Promptly after dinner we return to school. Cass, the other volunteer teachers, and a class of students have prepared a special welcome party in my honor.

We enter the room and the students stand and say in unison, "Welcome to our class!" The desks have been stacked in the back of the room, all the chairs arranged around the room on three sides. Ken and I are given seats at the front. Each student stands in turn to give their Chinese and English names and a brief greeting. In later reflections I marvel that I am almost assuredly the first non-Chinese person with whom they have ever spoken English. After I give a brief introduction and draw a terrible map of the States on the blackboard, the real fun begins.

The volunteer teachers have a host of activities planned, all of them focusing on honoring the guest. Several games involving balloons keep us warm in the unheated classroom, followed by a sweet song by a young girl. An older boy teaches me how to do a Chinese paper-cut and we produce beautiful red snowflakes. Many of the students come forward to present gifts to me. In terms of monetary value, I'm sure I have spent more on one rib dinner at the Outback than they did on all of the gifts combined. But my new knowledge of their situation from the afternoon visits radically changes my perspective and my heart feels heavy with emotion.

In the half-light of the hallway, Ken and I step into our abode for the night, our breath curling from our mouths. We slip off our shoes and thrust our feet into cold, hard plastic slippers. We brush our teeth using bottles of water purchased at a small store on the street. Ken asks me what I thought of the day.

"I'm overwhelmed. The kids are beautiful, so full of joy despite difficult conditions. And their hearts are so generous."

"Yeah, they really know how to be happy with less," he says.

The next morning we walk back to the school under a cold gray sky. We have slept well enough, despite the cold. Because it's Saturday, we arrive before most of the students are awake and play badminton with a few students in the courtyard in front of Cass's apartment. This morning we are going to take an excursion into the countryside.

This time we walk through town. We pass vegetable sellers with their greens laid out on tables or in baskets. Slabs of pork lie out on tables or hang on hooks. Shops have been open for a while now, and the town is buzzing with weekend activity. Ken grabs my arm and silently points to our left. A man is walking out of a public latrine with a shoulder-pole from which dangle two very full buckets of "stuff." He's taking the "stuff" to his field for fertilizer. Ken makes a face that speaks louder than words, and we laugh to assuage the seriousness of the situation. In all likelihood we may eat his vegetables, or ones like them, for dinner.

Today, because we're closer to town, we walk on a newly poured concrete road. Our first stop is a young man's brick home. As usual, we gather around a pile of hot ashes in a concrete fire ring, pass around plates of seeds and pieces of Chinese bread, and drink tea. Next we hike 400 meters up a hill. At the top sits a small thriving temple, about the size of a large walk-in closet. A monk dressed in orange robes sits outside a cinder-block residence, selling incense and fireworks. One of the full-time teachers at the middle school buys some incense and offers it to the Chinese god of wealth, bowing with his whole body and touching his forehead to the floor. An elderly lady motions for me to do the same. I politely refuse. I wish that I could communicate my confidence in the hope that I have, but my tongue fails me.

That afternoon nearly 200 students gather in a large auditorium built as a joint effort by contributions from Wuhan University and some large industries. Cass acts as translator for my self-introduction. We do several English activities to give the students opportunities to speak, and I walk around the room participating with them. Although the students are excited to have a lesson with a foreigner, I can see in their eyes that they know our time together will not ultimately benefit them greatly.

Over dinner that evening Cass explains the student situation in the countryside a little more.

"The school sometimes holds special events, giving away gifts and throwing parties to attract students to school. If they don't, many students won't come, especially the boys."

"But isn't school mandatory up through high school in China?" I ask.

"No. Right now education is compulsory through ninth grade. But the students know that after they graduate they will not be able to get into a university. Last year, one student was able to make it into a university, and three made it into vocational colleges. But over a hundred graduated. They know it's hopeless. They think it's better to start working and earning money now because when they graduate, they will be in the same situation as if they hadn't been in school."

"So how much help is it to learn English? Will they ever use it?"

"Not much really. It might give them a little hope. There are a few students who really study hard and we are hopeful that they'll get into university, but most of them will never use English for more than classroom work," says Cass.

Very early the next morning Cass, Ken, and I are standing under the school flag pole in the large courtyard. I have been asked to give the Monday morning encouragement speech to the students, normally given by the Headmaster. My words seem to flutter away on the cold breeze, as Cass translates my best attempt at a culturally appropriate pep talk. How can I have anything to say to them when I spend six times their family's annual income in one trip home in the summer?

After breakfast, a select number of high school students gather in the auditorium. This meeting is a special privilege, and only the more promising and dedicated students are allowed to attend. Even with the special selection, there are more students than the seats can hold and the aisles are packed, with students standing along the back wall. We play games that require basic language skills like Simon Says and a few English exercises I prepared beforehand.

The afternoon, when the winter weather is the warmest, is set aside for outdoor activities. Many of the boys are running up and down the basketball courts or standing on the sidelines cheering. Small groups of students collect around the ping pong tables or play badminton wherever a small open space can be found. A tug-of-war competition between classes draws the attention of a couple hundred students, cheering loudly for their friends.

After dinner with the volunteer teachers and the school official who arranged my visit, Cass tells me they have something special planned.

"We won't have any lectures this evening. But several of the classes would like you to come and teach them an English song. Because it's close to Christmas, I think maybe you can teach them a Christmas song?" It's asked as a question, but it's more of a statement of what I should do.

As I walk into the first classroom, I understand the surprise. Each student has a six-inch candle glowing on their desk. The lights have been turned off. Over one hundred faces reflect a warm, orange glow, dispelling the darkness.

On the blackboard I write out the words to the first verse of my favorite song "O Come, O Come, Emmanuel." I explain the words, and Cass translates. I sing through the verse and walk the students through it, word by word, note by note. By the third time, everyone is singing in full voice and I no longer sing with them, but drink in the warmth of the young voices.

After an hour and a half in three classrooms, my vocal chords are rubbing together and sounding as though I've been smoking for thirty years. The last bus back to Wuhan will leave soon, but Cass, hoping to give a few more classes an opportunity to sing, asks if I can go to a few more classrooms and sing for them before we leave.

Several classes and forty minutes later, with ragged voices and peaceful spirits, Ken and I say our last goodbyes. Cass accompanies us to the bus station. With tears in his eyes, he thanks us for coming.

"It's really been my pleasure, Cass. I am the one who has been blessed by your students. Thank you for giving me the opportunity to come here."

According to cultural custom, Cass won't let me "win" and insists that *they* were the ones most grateful, that I did so much for the students. But I know, in the lavishness with which they welcomed me into their homes and in their generosity and abundance of gifts, that I was the one served.

Ken and I take our seats in the front of the bus and I slip my mp3 player on again. I dial through the songs, looking for one that fits my mood.

16

The Stacks

by Sheryl Smalligan

THERE THEY ARE—FOUR TALL stacks of them, one stack for each class—sitting on that conveniently paper-width windowsill, taunting me, haunting me. I bare my teeth, stick my fingers in my ears, do my cat hiss, and grimace back.

I try to pretend they aren't there, but when I open my eyes, they have not shifted a millimeter, still so solidly sitting there. So I kill a few more minutes by counting them out into crisscross stacks of ten. Then I take the first ten essays and head into the fifty hours of blear-eye it will take to process the lot, trying not to remember that I also have lesson plans to ponder, students to meet, and a PowerPoint to create before class time next week.

Bring on the coffee!

When I retired in 2003 after thirty-plus years of teaching literature and writing in the U.S., I exulted, "I'll never grade another paper!" Then, without considering for more than five minutes, my husband and I took on teaching English to graduate students at Peking University (Beijing) in 2005, which we did for five semesters over the next five years.

What provoked a supposedly sane, middle-aged, "retired" high school teacher to take on such an assignment? Having spent a career reading student papers, I cannot claim I didn't know what I was getting into.

Yet something kept pulling me back—it continues to pull today. It must be that masochistic mix of pain and pleasure. Hours of tedium, yes—but also flashes of wonder and delight at what my students are thinking and writing. What an education it has been!

It has been an education in all those things teachers learn and re-learn. I have learned there are no shortcuts in teaching writing. For me to see my students develop in their writing skills, I have to read their work myself. For me to know what they're thinking, I have to read their work myself. So for me as a writing teacher, it's the old ball and chain of read and comment, read and comment, for as long as it takes. While I will not mark every peccadillo of punctuation and style in these papers now on my lap, I will carefully read each and "teach" with each, a commitment of about fifteen minutes or more for each paper that will totally tie up my weekend and other "own" time. A writing teacher soon learns that there is no "own" time during a semester.

I learn once again that, whether in the U.S. or in China, to teach how to write is to teach how to think. To write well is to think well—to write clearly is to think clearly. Students learn that in writing out their thoughts and organizing them, they are clarifying and developing what they think in ways they otherwise would not. As they write, students see themselves as thinking people with thoughts worth communicating. Substantive writing instruction goes way beyond teaching where to place the commas or how to use an adjective clause in stylistically effective ways. Correctness—those twenty-three rules about comma placement, for instance—is not all. It's not even the beginning of good writing instruction.

So students write and write and write—and I read and read and read. And as the semester goes along, their writing becomes more and more standard. Practice and imitation—not rules review—makes (more) perfect. I have learned to relax and let growth happen.

Meanwhile, as I ponder, I'm still looking at that first subset of ten essays, along with all their brothers and sisters and cousins.

There is plenty to smile about in these essays. The wonder of teaching writing in China is that growth is so easy to see. Not only growth in communicating thoughts more clearly—but also growth in confidence. Students may not be perfect writers at the end of the semester, but they are more confident writers. I see students progress from no confidence (all that self-effacing "My English is so bad") to a sure "I surprise myself! I can do it." At the beginning of the semester they are overwhelmed, in the middle they are crabby, at the end they are euphoric.

Yes, I love teaching writing in China.

But back to those papers. They sit there still, and they will sit there until I do something about them. My writing teacher fantasy has always been that someone will steal my stacks of papers. I have even left them on the front seat of my car with the door unlocked. Oh, false hope.

In these papers I see myself as a teacher. I also see the other half of that transaction—my extraordinary students. They come at me in large groups, large classes, in China, sitting there like forty-five eggs in a forty-five-egg-hole carton, desks bolted to the floor. And yet, by mid-semester, the blur of students resolves into separate and unique individuals, each one with something to teach me. I come away with my misconceptions inverted and my insights into Chinese culture clarified.

But those stacks of papers are still there—as a teacher I must, must read them. But when I position myself as a learner, I see what a treasure of creative insight and information they offer. How much I have learned from them that I would never have learned in any other way!

I quickly learn what topics invite open, personal writing. I am shocked with the willingness of my Chinese students to share themselves, once they see that I value their writing and that I expect more than stock responses.

I learn about customs—favorite regional foods, favorite restaurants, favorite traditions, the must-see spots in Beijing and in their hometowns. Their papers and journals become my guidebook and culture primer.

I read papers about the hot topics of the day, for example, living together before marriage (widely accepted), weddings (the registration, not the ceremony, is important), children and the one-child policy. About life directions and about uncertainty, about continuing education (nothing else to do), about continuing in a major not enjoyed (often assigned). About family histories, including traumatic experiences during the Cultural Revolution. About the Communist Party—a love/hate relationship in which students acknowledge the Party has brought China a long way but remain cynical about its corruption and arbitrariness. About nationalism. I've seen how government-controlled media manipulate students by nurturing a knee-jerk response to be turned on and off as needed on issues like Tibet, Japan, Taiwan. My students teach me about the internal politics of China through their responses—sometimes they are skeptical, too often credulous. Can I generalize on their responses? No. We in the West stereotype China as monolithic and thought-controlled. Yet opinions in China are as diverse as its diverse population, and my diverse students opine with surprising frankness. These papers are invaluable in learning about China from the inside. They are a cross-section of what its young people are thinking today.

Where else could I encounter such a cross-section of opinion and information as in my own classroom! But to return to my role as a teacher in reading those papers. . .

As always, the teacher becomes sometimes the counselor, sometimes the friend, sometimes the critic and encourager—one role shades into the others. Students will write what they will not say, and this is where those stacks of essays become a rare gift. Students are so eager to share. I am eager to be shared with.

So those stacks of papers also represent relationships. There may be over 150 papers in those stacks, and I wince at the effort it takes to read each one and respond to it. Yet each essay is a person, a person like no other on this earth, a person whose way now crosses mine, a person for whom I now have some responsibility.

I see another side to that shy boy, to that extrovert of a girl. Each paper is a letter to me, even though it may not be structured as such. Each one is a personal transaction—Teacher, look at me! See who I am!

Conversations that begin with a class assignment or a personal conference/coffee time continue via journal and email, some since our stay in Wuhan in 2003 and others from our years at Peking University. Students become friends. A call to meet for coffee—an invitation to dinner—pictures of students and other Peking University memorabilia on every shelf in our apartment.

Relationships develop—trust develops. I have been so privileged to help shape these young scholars, these wonderful young people.

But the stacks are still there—I despair at ever getting to the bottom, yet I also expect to learn something new, always something new.

Teaching in China has taught me humility.

I first came into China six years ago as a "foreign expert"—these were the actual words on a sign greeting us at our first hotel. I laughed— me, an expert?!—but unfortunately it's easy to embrace this chance to let the ego blossom. But we, of the advanced but not necessarily enlightened West, are not experts at all. We are foreigners who see only the surface of this culture and who often do not dig beneath. On the surface, how the Chinese do things seems often strange and funny to us. And yes, it sometimes is. I've done my share of eye-rolling, but I hope less now than

I did six years ago. Yes, we laugh, but we need to laugh privately and discerningly. Better, we need to understand why the differences exist and learn to appreciate them.

Our students chuckle at us too, their foreign teachers. How I wish I could see myself through their eyes. I hope I could chuckle too. Teaching in China has enabled me to stand back from my own culture and identify some of our locked-in attitudes, mine too.

I have learned political humility. Communism as an economic system is not as evil as purported during my growing-up years in the U.S., nor is democracy the faultless good that we presume.

As a system, democracy depends on long-standing and well-developed traditions such as rule of law and distribution of wealth through government entitlements to the less successful—traditions which modern China has not yet had time to develop as it manages its cumbersome population. I have come to appreciate the gargantuan task of governing such an unwieldy nation as China and of moving it into the twenty-first century. The Communist Party has brought China along the road to economic world power, and for that it has the respect of many (not all) of our Chinese students, many of whom are active Party members. My first shock—to realize that Communists could be such nice people!

We Westerners use "Communism" as a buzzword for lack of rights and brutal regimes, but we should remember that Communism also expresses high and elusive ideals, similar to those of Christianity. Also, we Westerners advance "rugged individualism" and a democratic (divisive) spirit as the desired antitheses to Communism, failing to see that "common" purpose better fits Chinese cultural norms and maybe ours as well. Maybe we advance our traditional values too forcefully. Maybe we should take a closer look at some of these Asian social values, such as harmony and unselfishness and personal meekness.

We Westerners often think we have all the answers to Third World problems, but nothing in China is as clean and simple as it looks from the Western perspective only. We wonder why the Chinese are so accepting and malleable, but we no longer wonder when we look to Confucianism, which urges acceptance of the political status quo or we see the five thousand years of dynastic rule, of looking to the top to lead and to solve problems. And we have to acknowledge the successes of the Party's top-down, managerial, "scientific" style. Chinese in general believe that human and societal perfection are attainable through human effort—hence, for many, an unwarranted faith in human reason and a failure to reckon with human sin and greed and massive corruption. My students' papers drive me to these realizations and also to further study.

And to deeper humility. We expats in China cannot fault the Chinese without noticing how our flaws mirror theirs. We see, for instance, that China's government and civic life in general run on "gray" money under the table, but then we must admit that our own "enlightened" system also pretends not to notice legalized bribery by lobbies, political graft, and use of power to manipulate the media. As in China, we see our own people looking increasingly to the government to ease their individual ways, exchanging votes not for wise governance but for ever more entitlements.

Have I become a cheerleader for the Chinese government? No. I appreciate my own culture and my own government, with its checks and balances and freedom of the press. But I have left behind that knee-jerk American tendency to redline anything labeled "Communist."

I have learned economic humility.

Of course, what U.S. citizen has not learned this, now that the U.S. has thoroughly embarrassed itself by generating the current economic woes worldwide? We cannot prate the success of our system underwritten, as it is, by Chinese loans. Capitalism, China understands—also "free" enterprise, as long as it works. The Chinese have an advantage in that the one-party government can manage both "private" and state-owned entities at will, without political gridlock, and can quickly change policies that aren't working. We in the U.S. may envy this efficiency as we struggle with the 2009 economic crisis and health programs.

We blame run-away laissez-faire industrialism for product recalls on Chinese goods. But who blames the U.S. importers of Chinese goods who insist on a bottom line that is below any realistic figure and achieved only by cutting corners and by sweatshop labor (the pros and cons of which are not so simple either)? We read about tainted milk in China. I return to the U.S. and find that peanut butter products and alfalfa sprouts are being recalled. Our newspaper runs a weekly list of recalls. Safety standards are higher here in the U.S. and more evenly enforced, yes, but not so reliable that we can afford to sneer at China.

I have become religiously more humble.

I believe God comes to the human race through Christ, not through Buddha or Laotzu, and I am willing to share with students that

Christianity is the only religion in which God comes to us in love and reconciliation—rather than our having to approach "the deities" with fear and appeasement. But I no longer see Buddhism or Taoism or Confucianism as incompatible with Christianity. I have learned to see these other religions as manifestations of the human search for God. I have learned to respect all such searching and to pray that all sincere searching for God—in whatever way—will lead to true knowledge and being "found." I leave God to work in mysterious ways.

I also see that love is not the private domain of Christians, as in "They will know we are Christians by our love." I certainly hope we Christians attract through our love, but I have met many wonderful non-Christian Chinese (and Americans and Japanese) who love much and who love well, shaming many Christians. Nor do we need to teach moral values to the Chinese. My students show me over and over that non-Christian cultures can have solid moral systems. In fact, they question as much as we do the moral content of the major U.S. export—pop culture. And at the same time, some of them fall into the deplorable moral habits of Western movies and music.

These are complex issues, and I can only suggest lines of discussion here. There are so many things one sees by stepping outside of one's culture. I am grateful to have had that chance. And much of whatever scant knowledge I have of the rich and complex and fascinating culture of China has come from reading the papers my students write.

Yes, I have loved teaching writing to my Chinese students. They have taught me so much more.

But back to those papers. In the moment, I still procrastinate and grumble and resent the hours I must spend. But they won't read themselves, so, energized by these perspectives, I pick up the first ten. I know I will want to keep a copy of each one.

17

Words

言

by Aminta Arrington

A man hath joy by the answer of his mouth:
and a word spoken in due season, how good is it!
—Proverbs 15:23, King James Bible

Water and words are easy to pour but impossible to recover.
—Chinese proverb

THERE IS SOMETHING ABOUT the mouth that seems to invite imagery and metaphor. Rivers and caves have mouths. Bottles and cannons have mouths. The Bible often invokes imagery of mouths. When Korah led a rebellion against Moses, the Bible tells us that "the earth opened its mouth and swallowed them up."[1] In the Psalms, God says, "I am the Lord your God, who brought you up out of Egypt. Open your mouth wide and I shall fill it."[2] And in the children's favorite, the story of Daniel in the lion's den,

words

---

1. Numbers 26:10.
2. Psalm 81:10.

Daniel tells us that "My God sent his angel, and he shut the mouths of the lions."[3]

Mouths are used in numerous idiomatic expressions in our English language. We describe one with a legacy of wealth as "born with a silver spoon in his mouth." Someone who utters embarrassing words is "putting his foot in his mouth." When surprised by someone of like mind, we exclaim, "You took the words right out of my mouth!" The Chinese language also acknowledges this relationship between a mouth and words. The Chinese character meaning "words," 言, truly looks like words emanating upward from an open mouth.

I thought of this character as I kept an eye on my daughter at the playground. We were thawing out from winter and anxious to spend time outdoors again. Usually, when I picked up the children from school, we stayed awhile so they could play on the school grounds. That particular afternoon I watched Katherine as she played with one of her classmates. Unlike the open mouth the venerable Calligrapher had drawn, my daughter's mouth was pursed tightly shut, as if demonstrating physically the sense of muteness she felt. She waved wildly with her arms or pointed to where she wanted her friend to go. But no words accompanied her frenzied gestures.

It was a poignant scene, for Katherine's nature was to be never without words. If she was feeling something, it came out of her mouth. If she had an idea, she shared it immediately. Thoughts made only momentary pit stops on her brain before they continued to their final destination out of her mouth. Yet I had placed her in a situation that rendered her wordless, so contrary to her very persona.

My husband Chris and I discussed Katherine's frustration at her inability to communicate. We thought about trying to get a tutor for her, but wondered how that would fit that into our busy family routine. At my next tutoring session with Zhang, I sought her advice. I asked what she thought about our paying one of the kindergarten teachers to spend some time one-on-one with Katherine during the course of the day, deliberately teaching her the words she needed to know, instead of Katherine's trying to pluck out word meanings as they rushed by in a torrent of classroom instruction.

But Zhang shook her head. "The teachers are all so busy," she said. "Since there are only two teachers in each classroom and usually more

3. Daniel 6:22.

than forty students, they just don't have time to stop what they are doing and focus on only one. It would be very difficult."

I knew she was right. And even requesting such would be to ask for special privileges as foreigners, something we tried not to do. So we were left with no good remedies.

Later that week we were finishing up dinner, usually a disjointed affair in our apartment. Our living room was so small that the table was wedged against the wall and an easy chair. There were spaces for the three kids to eat, but that was it. Usually Chris ate in the bedroom by the computer, and I in the kitchen. I always felt guilty about our lack of family dinners, but the combination of our small living space and the fry-it-then-serve-it nature of Chinese cuisine made a family meal difficult to pull off for one of questionable homemaking skills like me. But that night was different. We didn't all sit around the table, but Chris took his plate and sat on the living room couch, and I joined him.

It was a noisy affair with all five of us together, each child more interested in talking than eating. As I watched the kids at the table, I noticed Andrew had a bruise on his forehead.

"Grace, did Andrew fall down at school?" I asked.

She reported back in an authoritative manner: "Yes, Andrew fell down. Then a *Chinese* boy tried to jump on him, but I put up my hands and blocked him."

I looked at Chris. We chuckled at her rancor, for it seemed incongruous to hear Grace, adopted from China three years earlier, tell of how she had protected Andrew from the *Chinese* boy. "Doesn't she realize she's Chinese too?" we thought.

But quickly the reality of this little comment settled in. When Grace said the "Chinese" boy, she was saying this in a negative fashion. Where had she heard this? From her parents. We realized that quite often, in the course of telling each other about our day, words about the "Chinese people" figured into our stories somehow, usually when recounting our little frustrations.

Earlier that week Chris had said, "I was standing in line at the supermarket and a Chinese man cut right in front of me."

I recalled an earlier trip to the park and later telling Chris about it: "A whole group of Chinese people gathered around and stared at us, and some older Chinese ladies kept trying to grab Andrew's hair."

Or "These Chinese plastic bags (or insert another item that had just torn, or broken, or fallen apart) aren't worth anything. This one just got a hole in it."

In every case, our choice of words had created a negative image of people or things Chinese.

Had Grace gotten the idea that when we talked about a "Chinese" person we were downgrading that person with our speech? Her comment gave us insight into something we were doing, albeit unconsciously.

"Why did I even add the word 'Chinese'?" Chris asked himself out loud. "Of course the man who cut in front of me was Chinese. We're in China."

We were ashamed that in the frustration we sometimes experience living here, we had resorted to labeling. And we realized that by adding the word "Chinese" we were automatically dividing people into "them" and "us." We were making a distinction.

This eye-opening was particularly painful because one of the main reasons we came to China was to give Grace pride in being Chinese. We wanted her to enjoy a firmly implanted identity and to know where she came from. This incident showed us our careless remarks were doing the opposite of what we had intended. I hoped we could rectify it before this idea seeped deeper into her consciousness.

How I wished I could take those words back. But like the black marks used above the mouth by the Calligrapher in his interpretation of "words," 言 , once uttered, they remained.

~~~

The Chinese took 言 and used it as a radical to form many other characters that have words as an integral part of their meaning, such as "language" 語, "speech" 話, "poem" 詩, and "thanks" 謝謝.[4] But in the classroom, I learned a few more terms that the Calligrapher visibly viewed as rooted in words: "mistake," depicted as 誤, and "taboo", shown as 諱.[5]

---

4. In the course of simplification 言 remained unchanged, but characters that used 言 as a radical shifted to a simplified version; for example, 語 became 语. For this chapter, I used the traditional characters, for they kept the image of the words much more than the simplified version.

5. 諱 is the traditional version, still used in Taiwan and Hong Kong. When China simplified its characters, 諱 became 讳.

The word "taboo" leapt into the English language from the journals of Captain Cook,[6] who in the 1770s visited the Friendly Islands east of Fiji (now Tonga). It was originally used in an anthropological sense to describe forbidden customs, or sacred items consecrated for special use. The Chinese word, with its 言 radical, foreshadowed what the English term would gradually come to mean: sensitive topics which we tried to avoid talking about.

ERRC, our sponsoring organization, advised us to stay clear of contentious issues, particularly Taiwan. I felt I understood the Chinese point of view that Taiwan was an integral part of "one China," so I was completely taken aback when my sophomores and I had an incident over Taiwan. I read the following sentence out of their textbook: "Since the mid-1980s, Japan, South Korea, Taiwan, and Thailand have all succumbed to pressure from Washington and allowed the sale of foreign-brand cigarettes."

At this point I paused.

"Do you know all these countries?" I asked, just to make sure they were aware of the English names for these geographical places.

There was immediate commotion.

"Which country don't you know?" I asked.

"They are not all *countries*!" they indignantly replied.

Then I realized my error. Lumping Taiwan together with the other three and labeling them all as "countries," was taboo, 諱, a blasphemy they had caught immediately. I rolled my eyes and said:

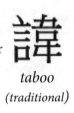

taboo
(traditional)

"Oh, I'm sorry. What I meant to say was, 'Do you know these three countries and one Chinese renegade province?'"

They nodded approvingly.

Later in the course, we had a unit on diplomacy, and as part of the lesson I showed them a map of Asia so we could review the English names for all the countries. As I was speaking, I noticed that while mainland China was the color yellow, on this map the island of Taiwan stood out in pink. I pointed this out to the students, making a passing remark that in the West we had a different view of Taiwan: while it may not be its own country, it was somehow separate from the PRC.

---

6. Published in 1777 as *A Voyage of the Pacific Ocean*.

This was a mistake, a 誤, as the Calligrapher styled it. To so offhandedly make such a remark to my students, wound up after years of indoctrination over the Taiwan issue, only inflamed them. As the Calligrapher wisely knew, most mistakes have a great amount to do with opening our mouths. In this case, he added a second mouth to the character just to underline the point.

mistake
(traditional)

I began to go on from the map exercise, but one of the male students, Roy, raised his hand. Roy, like most of the boys, had never been particularly vocal in class. But at that moment he felt compelled to stand up and give me a formal speech demarcating the history of Taiwan and its relationship to the mainland, concluding of course, that Taiwan was intrinsically part of China.

He was immediately followed by another student who wished to elaborate on points Roy had made. Altogether four students, three of them male students—normally quiet in class and usually speaking only to inform me they had to miss class for soccer matches—stood up to give speeches. This was not a political issue; it was a personal issue, deeply personal.

They were deeply resentful at U.S. "interference" when they felt there had been a chance to regain Taiwan some decades ago and felt the continued separation had reinforced China's "weak" status, a label that would not be removed until Taiwan was back in the fold. It was an open wound not just on the country, but on themselves. Except perhaps for the 9/11 attacks, in my lifetime I have never known Americans to be so personally affected by international relations. China's history, particularly its recent history involving weakness, capitulation, and embarrassment at the hands of the West, was completely intertwined with the personal self-esteem of my students.

On the break, Lois, who had been to my house and taught me to make hot and sour potatoes, came over to chat.

"In my mind, the issue of Taiwan is the biggest international relations issue facing the Chinese government today. Only when this issue is put to rest, in a satisfactory manner of course, will we Chinese finally be able to restore our national pride."

During the speeches, the name Chiang Kai-shek had come up many times, usually spat out. Lois said she had a different view. "In a way, he was a patriot, for it was never his intent to separate Taiwan from China.

Rather, he fled to Taiwan hoping to regroup and eventually govern all of China. Now, so many years later, although neither the Communists nor Chiang Kai-Shek desired it, Taiwan has been separated."

"But in those years, Taiwan has achieved economic prosperity and rather enjoys being separate," I told her.

"But for the mainland, the family can never truly be happy until the wayward son has returned home," she replied.

～～～

On a Saturday a few weeks later, I took the children to the kindergarten playground. Again, a classmate was there. This time Katherine, to my complete surprise, chatted away happily with her friend.

The other parents around us chuckled and looked at me with surprise. "She speaks Chinese!"

I nodded in astonished agreement.

At one point her friend fell down and Katherine's words tumbled out as she comforted her with a long complex Chinese sentence, which she then roughly translated for me as "Don't worry about it, you'll be fine."

Grace and Andrew picked up the cue from their older sister, and the three of them began using more and more Chinese with one another at home, including the occasional insult, thinking their parents couldn't understand them.

"*Wo zui hao, ni chao hao,*" Katherine would say to Grace. "I'm the best. You're the worst."

"I understand you," I'd say sternly, whether I did or not. No matter what language they used, the surly tone translated easily.

Our children's language range remained limited, as they were only exposed to schoolchild Chinese. They would continue to learn as their context expanded. But I was thrilled with their progress, particularly Katherine's. This had been a long road for her and for us, but we now felt that all three children had a strong foothold in this language that would serve as a foundation for the years to come. From that beginning, when the mouth finally opened, the words flowed faster and faster, every day and every week, freely and naturally—just as the Calligrapher had imagined.

Contributor Biographies

Aminta Arrington has been in Tai'an, China with her husband Chris and their three children for four years. She is a graduate of Johns Hopkins University School of Advanced International Studies. She first felt a connection with Chinese culture when she studied Japanese (which uses Chinese characters), and the connection deepened when she and Chris adopted daughter Grace from Jiangxi Province in 2004.

Don Barnes has been in China for seven years, which is enough time to have gained a strange appreciation for Peking Opera and hot pepper sauce, and to want to stay as long as possible. His one negative culinary experience was when he somehow accidentally dropped his plate into a squat toilet.

Karen Barnes has been in China for seven years, and taught ESL for eighteen years before arriving. She steers clear of Peking Opera, early-morning jackhammers, and other annoying sounds. Like her husband Don, she plans to be in China as long as possible.

Emily Ciccotti is in the middle of her fourth year in China, first in Nanchang, then Changsha, and currently Wuhan. She hopes to extend indefinitely, with a hiatus for her husband to finish his Ph.D. Her desire to stay so long in China might be motivated by her having already served a year in the substitute teaching trenches just before leaving America.

Jesse Ciccotti is currently studying Chinese at Wuhan University, where he previously taught English for four years. While in Wuhan he has developed a culinary appreciation for snakeskin, but has never developed an appetite for *chou doufu* (stinky tofu). While he wasn't particularly interested in China when he first arrived, he now has a great love for China and once he earns his Ph.D. in philosophy, plans to stay for a lifetime.

Pamela Holt took a short-term missions trip to China in 2000 while a faculty member at Westmont College. Just two months later she re-signed her job and moved to China where she has been ever since, teaching Chemistry at Shandong University. She has surprisingly few DVDs (50) for such a long stay, has learned to hate cuckoos after being woken up by them too many times to count, and hopes to never again eat silkworms.

Amanda Hostetler has lived in Wuhan since 2008 with her husband and five of her children, where she is the English Department coor-dinator for the SMIC primary school. Her interest in China comes by way of her two (soon to be three) adopted Chinese children. Her interaction with Chinese cuisine is generally positive, with the exception of chicken feet, though if her children had their way the family would only dine at McDonald's.

Lindsey Paulick is a graduate of Western Seminary in Portland, Oregon, and taught for one year at Baoding in Hebei Province. In that time she experienced many of the unique joys of China, includ-ing traveling in cramped conditions (six hours on a minibus with her knees at her chest), televised Peking Opera, and the gratitude all foreigners feel when they see McDonald's, or more specifically, see their bathrooms.

Robert Moore has been involved in China off and on since a summer trip in 2001. He has taught in Tai'an, Tianjin, and Beijing. Currently he is studying for his master's degree in Chinese literature at Nankai University in Tianjin. He loves Chinese food, with a few major ex-ceptions, chief among them being pig face, a dish he was served in Shandong Province, which still had the hair on it.

Sheryl Smalligan became interested in China when her son, who had been in China for several years, married a Chinese colleague. She has taught in China off and on since 2003, splitting time between China and America. She has ridden for 25 hours in the hard-seat section of a train from Xinjiang to Xi'an, has hosted a Chinese girl in America who practiced Peking Opera in her basement (which some would say was worse than the train ride), and once ordered shrimp without adding the word for "plate," which resulted in her receiving a single shrimp on a large plate.

Daniel Jaime has been teaching in Tai'an, China for four and a half years, before which he braved a one-month ESL training course which tested his mettle and his mind, and plans to stay in China long-term. He has compiled a collection of almost 157 DVDs, is enthusiastic about the fact that every year there's something new in China, but is less than excited about yappy dogs and loud exercise music outside his window in the morning, and has avoided the north gate of his university for weeks in order to stay clear of the smell of *chou doufu* (stinky tofu).

Samara Sanchez has taught in China for close to five years. In addition to teaching at Beijing Language and Culture University, she is involved in numerous social projects around Beijing, particularly those aimed at helping young migrant women. She is well-versed in many of the odder parts of Chinese culture, having taken numerous marathon train trips and eaten sandworms.